Early Praise for Test iOS Apps with UI Automation

Jonathan Penn is the perfect person to teach you how to test your iOS apps with UI Automation. He is passionate about testing and has a lot of experience both in iOS development and in the JavaScript required to make your tests sing. This book is filled with techniques you'll use immediately to make your iOS apps more robust.

➤ Daniel Steinberg, Dim Sum Thinking

Automated testing is essential to delivering quality software. In this book Jonathan lays out the details of how to use the UI Automation tools to build a test suite that will keep your app in tip-top shape.

➤ Bill Dudney

Automated testing is a technique that every developer can benefit from. It's a dry topic, but Jonathan is able to bring clarity, comedy, and context to a very useful though poorly documented tool.

➤ Josh Smith

Web-to-mobile converts often find it challenging to bring their automated-testing habits with them, due in part to the fact that touch gestures and native UI widgets are much harder to expose to automated testing than HTTP requests and HTML output. Apple's UI Automation is a big step in the right direction in this regard, but it takes the guidance of a pioneer like Jonathan Penn to assemble a full repertoire of developer tools to extend the reach of Apple's tools and achieve a high level of code confidence.

➤ Chris Adamson

My iOS development knowledge has been raised a notch by reading this book. It's great that I could take my existing JavaScript skills and learn how to apply them to the field of iOS testing. I'll definitely be using these techniques on the next app I build!

➤ **Stephen Orr, lead developer, Made Media**

Being a big advocate of automated acceptance testing myself, in the past few years UI Automation has become my weapon of choice for iOS applications. Jonathan Penn is an absolute authority on the topic and his work has made my life easier too many times to count. Now whenever people ask for advice on the topic, I can just point them to this book, and it will answer all their questions and then some.

➤ **Alexander Repty**

Jonathan's book is the best I've read about building great automated tests for your iOS applications. The book has clear and comprehensive examples that help you understand how to write great tests for your own projects. Not only does he show you how to write solid tests; he shares best practices and techniques to maintain a test suite as it grows. If you want to go beyond unit tests and automate your app end-to-end, this book will get you started.

➤ **Shiney Rossi, senior mobile engineer, Nest Labs**

Jonathan Penn succeeds at opening up the world of UI Automation testing to everyone with his new book, *Test iOS Apps with UI Automation*. From acceptance testing to performance testing, *Test iOS Apps* covers all the steps to go from zero to a full suite of automated tests that will help make your apps better. Sit down and enjoy this engaging book to learn how to automate everything!

➤ **Conrad Stoll, software engineer, Mutual Mobile**

Test iOS Apps with UI Automation

Bug Hunting Made Easy

Jonathan Penn

The Pragmatic Bookshelf

Dallas, Texas • Raleigh, North Carolina

Many of the designations used by manufacturers and sellers to distinguish their products are claimed as trademarks. Where those designations appear in this book, and The Pragmatic Programmers, LLC was aware of a trademark claim, the designations have been printed in initial capital letters or in all capitals. The Pragmatic Starter Kit, The Pragmatic Programmer, Pragmatic Programming, Pragmatic Bookshelf, PragProg and the linking *g* device are trademarks of The Pragmatic Programmers, LLC.

Every precaution was taken in the preparation of this book. However, the publisher assumes no responsibility for errors or omissions, or for damages that may result from the use of information (including program listings) contained herein.

Our Pragmatic courses, workshops, and other products can help you and your team create better software and have more fun. For more information, as well as the latest Pragmatic titles, please visit us at *http://pragprog.com.*

The team that produced this book includes:

Brian P. Hogan (editor)
Potomac Indexing, LLC (indexer)
Candace Cunningham (copyeditor)
David J Kelly (typesetter)
Janet Furlow (producer)
Juliet Benda (rights)
Ellie Callahan (support)

Printed in the United States of America.
ISBN-13: 978-1-937785-52-9
Printed on acid-free paper.
Book version: P1.0—August 2013

Contents

Acknowledgments

First, I want to thank my inner circle of authors, who encouraged me to go through the pain to write a book in the first place. Daniel Steinberg, Bill Dudney, Joshua Smith, and Jason Gilmore—thank you. I would have been lost without your example and your terrifying stories.

Thanks to all who submitted feedback and errata throughout the beta process, and specifically those who slogged through the tech reviews and took the time to write up the awesome feedback: Chris Adamson, Heath Borders, Jayme Deffenbaugh, Jason Gilmore, Jeff Holland, Ben Lachman, Kurt Landrus, Kevin Munc, Mark Norgren, Stephen Orr, Julián Romero, Shiney Rossi, Joshua Smith, Daniel Steinberg, Conrad Stoll, Elizabeth Taylor, TJ Usiyan, and Alex Vollmer.

Thanks to CocoaConf for giving me all those opportunities to practice the material in this book—over and over.

Thanks to the team at The Pragmatic Programmers for the resources they provided and for letting me prove myself. Special thanks to my editor, Brian Hogan, for wisely convincing me to scrap the first draft of the book and for fielding my incessant questions.

To my parents, who fed my famished curiosity. To my daughter, Niah, who thinks I work at a coffee shop for a living. To my son, Ian, who thinks I know what I want to do when I grow up. And to my partner, Colleen. She put up with my swinging moods and sleepless nights and surely shed more sweat than I did.

For great justice.

Introduction

We iOS developers have a lot on our minds. We want to build useful and bug-free software for our customers while keeping up with Apple's fast pace. Software development is fraught with trade-offs and, unfortunately, testing our software is often traded away in the crunch time before a release date.

So what's the best way to hunt for bugs in our apps? We spend a lot of our own time manually launching and walking through the features one by one, tapping, swiping...over and over again. This book helps us find a better way.

What Can We Do About It?

Nothing will replace the spot-checking ingenuity of a human tester, but we can certainly automate the important common tasks and free ourselves up to focus on other things. We want to use automated tests to raise confidence while we keep forging ahead and to give us useful information when something goes wrong.

In this book, we're going to focus on testing by scripting interactions through the user interface. This is known as *full stack* or *integration* testing in some circles. We're launching the whole app, tapping and gesturing, waiting for animations, and reacting to results from the screen.

We're going to be strategic with how we apply these tests. Automation testing is a powerful way to smoke out bugs, but it's not without its limitations. These kinds of tests are slow and it's not feasible to test every edge case using this technique. We're not going to cover effective lower-level testing strategies such as unit tests—for more information about that, you'd want to read Graham Lee's book *Test-Driven iOS Development [Lee12]*, or Daniel Steinberg's book *Test Driving iOS Development With Kiwi [Ste12]*. Here, we're looking to test deep slices of the application while answering the question "Did we wire the components correctly?"

We have two ultimate goals with these tests. First, we want to verify correct behavior with *acceptance tests* that list the steps a user would take and the requirements to consider a feature complete. Second, we want to automate the mundane tasks involved in performance testing. Looking for memory leaks often involves walking through the app and doing the same thing over and over again while recording benchmarks. This is a perfect use case for automation.

Great, So How Do We Get There?

In these pages, we'll be focusing on *UI Automation*, a tool Apple provides that works out of the box and integrates with Xcode. We don't need to install anything to get started and try it out. It was first introduced in iOS 4 as part of Instruments, a robust tool to trace application behavior at runtime. Along with the rest of the instruments available to us, UI Automation gives us a lot of power to assert proper behavior and run extensive performance analysis through different usage scenarios.

Here's where we'll be going:

- Chapter 1, *UI Automation Overview*, on page 1, gets us started by walking through how to capture and play back in the simulator actions we perform on an app. We also take a moment to look at how UI Automation and Instruments work together.

- Chapter 2, *Testing Behavior with UI Automation*, on page 11, builds on the basics and leads you through writing a test that asserts a behavior in the app. We'll take a tour through the automation-scripting interface and learn how we can report failures in our tests.

- Chapter 3, *Building a Test Suite*, on page 23, walks through some simple techniques to start building up a suite of acceptance tests that run one after the other against the application. We'll continue exploring the UI Automation scripting interface and discuss how to group together output from various tests.

- Chapter 4, *Organizing Test Code*, on page 41, explains some good ways to grow our test code in a way that is readable and maintainable. We'll start pulling out reusable pieces into a testing toolbox that we can import anywhere we need it and represent portions of our application screen with special objects.

- Chapter 5, *Maps, Gestures, and Alerts*, on page 59, takes us on a journey underground to learn how UI Automation talks to our application. We'll trigger complex gestures on the map view, alter the way UI Automation sees the elements on the screen, and discuss how best to handle modal alert views.

- Chapter 6, *Strategies for Testing Universal Apps*, on page 79, walks through some scenarios that test the different idioms on iPhone and iPad screens. We'll start a separate suite of iPad acceptance tests while reusing all the testing tools we've built.

- Chapter 7, *Automating Performance Tests*, on page 101, uses the integrated power of UI Automation and Instruments to record benchmarks as the app runs through a variety of performance tests. If you've ever needed to tap, tap, tap over and over again to re-create a memory problem, you'll love this chapter.

- Chapter 8, *Setting Up Application Data*, on page 121, introduces concepts and ideas for bootstrapping the app data in a state that is ready for our tests. We'll discuss good app architectures that make this easier, and look at how environment variables and seed files can inject the information we need into the app at runtime.

- Chapter 9, *Stubbing External Services*, on page 147, helps us deal with the unpredictability of external services. We'll tackle some techniques to fake services at the network layer and even fork our Objective-C code to stub out more-complicated dependencies within the app.

- Chapter 10, *Command-Line Workflow*, on page 165, provides tips to run UI Automation tests from shell scripts. We'll be automating our automated tests, as it were.

- Chapter 11, *Third-Party Tools and Beyond*, on page 191, tours some third-party tools to use with the workflow we discuss in the book. We'll also review useful tools outside of the UI Automation sandbox.

By the end of the book, you'll have a great set of habits you can draw from when you're faced with the unique challenges in your applications.

Follow Along with the Source

Most apps are very complicated state machines with so many possibilities for error that it seems overwhelming. The network, database frameworks, animations, device orientation—all these external and internal dependencies conspire to give us quite a challenge.

We'll face these challenges while studying an actual app throughout the book. By growing a set of test tools based on the needs of a real app, we'll keep ourselves organized and learn to work around the quirks. The source is available for download from the book's website (http://www.pragprog.com/titles/jptios).

Here's the best way to follow along with the code. Each chapter gets its own top-level directory prefixed by the chapter number, like 06-Universal. Each chapter is broken into a series of steps. Every step directory is a complete copy of the app—a snapshot of what the book expects at that point. This is so that you can pick up anywhere in the book and everything will work (or not work if that's what we happen to be exploring). Each snippet of code referenced in this text is annotated to point to the step directory it comes from.

Expectations and Technical Requirements

This isn't a book for iOS beginners. We're going to dive deep into Xcode's build system, the Objective-C runtime, shell scripts, and more. I recommend starting with these books as prerequisite material:

- *iOS SDK Development [AD12]*, by Chris Adamson and Bill Dudney

- *iOS Recipes: Tips and Tricks for Awesome iPhone and iPad Apps [WD11]*, by Paul Warren and Matt Drance

- *Core Data: Apple's API for Persisting Data on Mac OS X [Zar12]*, by Marcus Zarra

I assume you've been through Apple's introductory material, know about how view controllers and memory-management work, and know how to build your own application in the Xcode GUI. We'll be working with at least Xcode 4.6 and iOS 6.1.

Good luck and happy bug-hunting!

CHAPTER 1

UI Automation Overview

Every time we add new features to our apps and fire up the simulator to make sure we didn't break anything, we're testing. Every time we tap on the same button over and over to see if we have a memory leak, we're testing. Testing software involves a lot of repetitive work, and repetitive work is excellent work for a computer to do.

Instead of manually tapping and swiping while looking for problems, we can build scripts that do these things for us. Automating our testing process is a long journey with a lot of opportunities and challenges, so we'll break it down into manageable chunks.

In this chapter, we'll start the journey by using Apple's built-in UI Automation tool to capture and play back a very simple script of user interactions. We'll get a glimpse of the tool's power and limitations, and we'll delve into the iOS project we'll be working with throughout the book as we build our tests one piece at a time.

NearbyMe is an app that keeps a list of frequently used search terms to find points of interest at your current location. It leverages the OpenStreetMap API to do the lookup and Apple's Map Kit framework to present results like we see in Figure 1, *NearbyMe*, on page 2.[1] It's a universal app that uses table views, network access, Core Location, and Core Data. This gives us a great playground to exercise a wide range of techniques for testing complex iOS applications. You can learn more about downloading and using the source code in *Follow Along with the Source*, on page xi.

---

1. http://www.openstreetmap.org/

Figure 1—NearbyMe

1.1 Capturing Our First Script from the Simulator

Let's jump right in and go through the motions to capture gestures in the simulator. This will get us used to the Instruments profiling tool that houses UI Automation, and will give us a script we can study to learn how it works. Follow along to get a feel for the workflow.

Does UI Automation Work on the Device?

Yes, it does! If you choose your device in Xcode, Instruments will launch and attach to the app running on the device instead.

Some differences between the simulator and device environments may matter for your own applications. The camera shows up only on the device, and some performance tests, such as CPU and GPU benchmarks, are best performed on devices.

But we're starting with the simulator because it is simpler to get going and it sets us up for a lot of flexibility later on. For this particular application, the behaviors we are going to test work the same on both platforms. And since the simulator is itself an app running on the Mac, we have more control, like triggering memory warnings or resetting it when we need it.

Open up the NearbyMe project in Xcode and make sure the latest iOS simulator SDK is selected in the upper-left corner of the Xcode window. We launch

Instruments by choosing Profile from the Product menu (or pressing ⌘I). Xcode will build the application for the Release configuration and launch Instruments.

Instruments then presents a template chooser showing off all the starting points for using it, as the following figure shows. We'll go into more detail about setting up your own templates in Chapter 7, *Automating Performance Tests*, on page 101. For our purposes right now, let's choose the default UI Automation template.

Figure 2—Instruments template chooser

Once selected, Instruments creates a new *trace document* from the template and launches the app in the simulator. It immediately begins recording a *trace* of the application. We want to start our capture from scratch, so stop the trace by clicking the red record button in the upper-left corner, as shown in Figure 3, *Stopping the Instruments trace*, on page 4.

We create a blank script in this document by clicking on the Add button in the left-hand sidebar and choosing Create from the pop-up menu, as shown in Figure 4, *Choosing to create a script*, on page 4.

Figure 3—Stopping the Instruments trace

Figure 4—Choosing to create a script

When we create the script; the bottom half of the window switches to a script editor, and we see the line in the following figure.

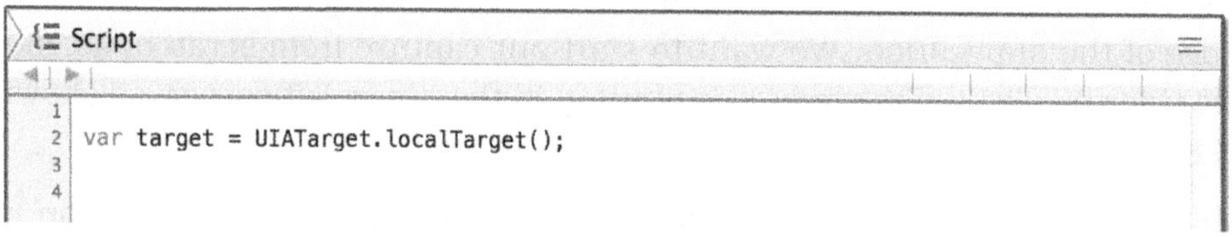

```
1
2 var target = UIATarget.localTarget();
3
4
```

Figure 5—The Instruments script pane

This script pane is our playground. We'll do most of our editing in here. It gives us a lot of nifty help through syntax highlighting and inline error messages when bad things happen. It's not perfect, but it's a good place to start learning.

UI Automation exposes everything to us through JavaScript. The first line grabs the target instance that represents the simulator the app is running on. The script editor always puts this line at the top of scripts it creates for us, because everything starts and goes through the target.

Let's practice capturing a script by tapping a few buttons to exercise the app's UI. We'll change the sort order and toggle the edit mode for the table view on and off—just enough activity to see something happen.

To launch the app and start capturing, click the red record button *at the bottom of the script pane.* Switch over to iOS Simulator, tap the By Name segmented control below the table view, then tap the Edit button in the navigation bar (see the following figure). Tap the By Recent segmented control below the table view to put the sort order back where it was, and then tap Done in the navigation bar to turn off the edit mode.

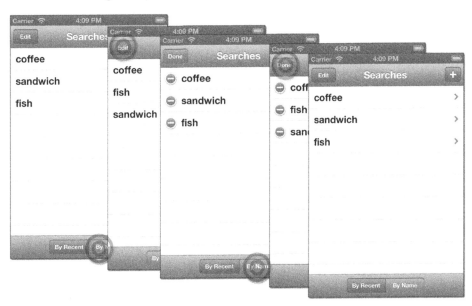

Figure 6—Playing back the script

With each action a line is appended to the script editor, showing us how UI Automation perceives the touch events it captures. Press the stop button *at the bottom of the script pane* when you're finished.

Now let's play back these actions by pressing the play button *at the bottom of the script editor*. The pane with the script editor switches to show an output log, and the tap events are played back in the app as we captured them.

That's it! We've just captured our first automation script. It doesn't yet assert any behavior we're expecting, but we're well on our way. Now that we've dipped our toes into the pool of UI Automation, let's pause to understand what we just did.

1.2 Finding Our Way around UI Automation

At first glance, UI Automation and Instruments together can be pretty overwhelming. In this section, we're going to take a step back and examine what we've been using. Instruments is primarily a profiling tool built on the idea of running and recording a *trace* of activity in an application.

The window we've been working in is a *trace document* where all the activities over the course of the application run are traced. The key components of the trace-document window are broken down in the following figure.

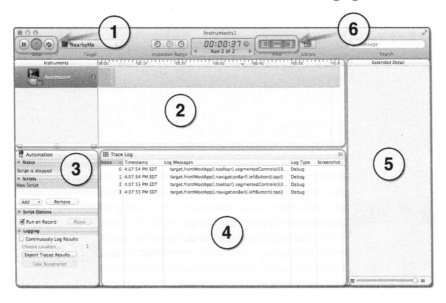

Figure 7—Getting to know Instruments

1. These buttons control the *trace recording* in Instruments. The red record button is the one we'll use the most. When it's pressed, Instruments runs and attaches to the target application and starts recording the trace. When it's pressed again, the application is terminated and the trace recording stops. Note that this is *not* the same as the red record button at the bottom of the script pane we used to capture a script.

2. This *track pane* is where all the instruments show up and give a graphical overview of what they observe during the trace. Right now we have only the UI Automation instrument, and we'll see green or red regions in the timeline depending on whether the tests pass or fail.

3. We use the left sidebar to command and control the UI Automation instrument. The Status section shows us the state of the automator, currently stopped. The Scripts section is where we manage sets of scripts to run inline. The Script Options area gives us execution control, like if we should automatically run a script when a trace recording begins. And the Logging section has to do with the automation trace logs that we'll get to later.

4. This lower pane is the heart of the automation instrument. Every time we play back an automation script, the pane switches to show the trace log, as we see here. We can switch back to the script pane by clicking the pop-up button named Trace Log at the top of the pane and choosing Script from the menu. There's also an undocumented shortcut to toggle between the script and trace-log panes by double-clicking on the text in the Status section of the left sidebar.

5. The right sidebar is where we'll see more details for individual items selected in the trace log. JavaScript exceptions or usage errors also show more detail here.

6. These toolbar buttons let us toggle the visibility of each of these panes. We can turn the sidebars off when we need more room.

Tweaking the Captured Script

Now let's dissect the script that came out of the recording; we'll switch back to the script pane so we see what's in Figure 8, *The recorder's initial output*, on page 8.

The captured automation script starts with the target object that represents the simulator, gets the frontmost application, and then drills down into the interface to identify which button will be tapped.

```
1
2   var target = UIATarget.localTarget();
3
4   target.frontMostApp().toolbar() .segmentedControls()[0]   .buttons()["By Name"]   .tap();
5   target.frontMostApp().navigationBar() .leftButton()   .tap();
6   target.frontMostApp().toolbar() .segmentedControls()[0]   .buttons()["By Recent"]   .tap();
7   target.frontMostApp().navigationBar() .leftButton()   .tap();
8   |
```

Figure 8—The recorder's initial output

A blue bubble means that there is more than one way to reference that element on the screen. UI Automation picked one that it thought was most suitable while capturing our actions, but we can click the disclosure triangle to choose a more meaningful one if we want. For example, we can change the reference to the left-hand button in the navigation bar to instead look up the button by the name Done, as the following figure shows.

```
1
2   var target = UIATarget.localTarget();
3
4   target.frontMostApp().toolbar() .segmentedControls()[0]   .buttons()["By Name"]   .tap();
5   target.frontMostApp().navigationBar() .leftButton()   .tap();
6   target.frontMostApp().toolbar() .segmentedControls()[0]   .buttons()["By Recent"]   .tap();
7   target.frontMostApp().navigationBar() .leftButton()
8                                                     ✓ leftButton()
                                                      buttons()["Done"]
                                                      buttons()[0]
                                                      elements()["Done"]
                                                      elements()[1]
```

Figure 9—Choosing the table view by index

Capturing scripts like this is a great way to practice exploring this scripting interface. If you're ever stumped on how to reach for a certain control or you want to see other ways to do it, capturing your actions can help.

Limitations of Capturing Actions

Unfortunately, the script-capturing mechanism has limitations, too. Sometimes it can have trouble finding buttons on the screen, or it can get confused when trying to record raw gesture events.

For example, we'll try tapping the + button in the app to add a new search term to the list. When we tap on it, an alert will pop up with a text field and show the onscreen keyboard (as the following figure shows). Let's capture these steps and see what happens.

Figure 10—Capturing actions involving alerts

Create a new script by choosing Add > Create in the script sidebar. Press the red record button at the bottom of the script pane, switch to iOS Simulator, and then tap the + button in NearbyMe's navigation bar. On your Mac keyboard, type the word coffee and then tap Add to create the search term. In Instruments, press the stop button beneath the script pane to see this captured script (shown in the figure here).

```
1
2  var target = UIATarget.localTarget();
3
4  target.frontMostApp().navigationBar() .rightButton()  .tap();
5  // Alert detected. Expressions for handling alerts should be moved into the
       UIATarget.onAlert function definition.
6  target.frontMostApp().alert() .defaultButton()  .tap();
7  |
```

Figure 11—Confusing the UI Automation script-capture mechanism

UI Automation balked when faced with the alert. We'll have to step in and do our own manual work to handle the alert and decide what to do. That can wait until Section 3.1, *Testing with a Modal Alert View*, on page 23. For the moment, just know that the capturing process isn't recording raw data for your *exact* steps and your timing as you perform them. It is trying to convert what you are doing into individual automation-script lines.

Beyond the Basics

Phew! That was a whirlwind tour of UI Automation and Instruments. We recorded some actions and stepped back to examine how we did it and what it produced. Try these techniques to capture and play back your actions as you poke around in your applications. What happens if you try to capture gestures such as swipes or pinches? You'll undoubtedly run into limitations like what we experienced here, but it's a great place to start and learn.

Capturing events can be a useful way to get up and running quickly, but if we're going to build long-living and quickly adapted test scripts, we must learn to write our own by hand. To take our UI Automation scripting to the next level, let's dig into the language and interface.

CHAPTER 2

Testing Behavior with UI Automation

We've learned a bit about how UI Automation functions, but the script we recorded doesn't do anything useful for us. Let's put UI Automation to work. We're going to write a simple *acceptance test* that focuses on verifying application behavior through the eyes of the users, what they do, and what they expect. Automated acceptance-test scripts are a great way to demonstrate that we know how a feature is supposed to work, and we can re-run them at any time to inform us if the feature breaks.

Let's start with something simple and write a test to make sure that the user is able to remove a search term from the list in our app, like we see in the following figure.

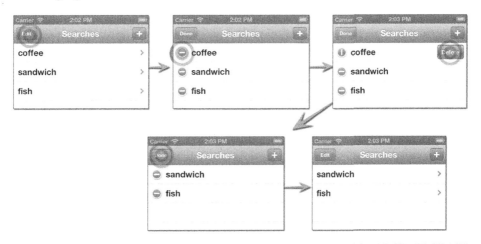

Figure 12—Deleting the "coffee" search term

To do this we'll need to know how to find the search-term cell on the screen, expose the Delete button, tap it, and then check to make sure that the cell is gone. Then we'll need to learn how to report a problem back to us. To make sure we're covering the feature like we claim to be, we'll check our work by purposely breaking the application and watching to make sure the test fails. When we're done, we'll have our first acceptance test!

2.1 Talking to the UI through JavaScript

To get the most out of UI Automation, we need to get to know the scripting interface. It exposes a bunch of objects to us that we query and manipulate as representations of the application and what the user experiences on the screen. We saw glimpses of this when we captured some simple actions back in Section 1.1, *Capturing Our First Script from the Simulator*, on page 2, but we're ready now to start writing our own by hand.

For better or worse, UI Automation uses JavaScript to do its magic. I know, I know, you're probably shuddering in fear from the horror stories you've heard when dealing with the cross-browser headaches in web development. Don't worry; it's not that bad here. This is an isolated JavaScript runtime. There's no document object model, and there's no ancient-browser compatibility to worry about.

The documentation on UI Automation is thorough but somewhat difficult to navigate if you don't know what you're looking for. You can search for it by choosing Documentation and API Reference from Xcode's Help menu, or view it on the Web.[1] We'll make the best use of it if we introduce ourselves first to some key objects and methods. In this section, we'll walk down the path of the scripting interface from the very top while we write our acceptance test for the behavior to remove a search term from the list.

Starting at the Top with UIATarget

Remember back to the captured script in Figure 8, *The recorder's initial output*, on page 8. When we call the UIATarget.localTarget() method, UI Automation retrieves an object representing the target we are working with. In this context, the target refers to the device or simulator on which the app is running. This is an unfortunate naming clash, since it often confuses beginners to think it has something to do with what Xcode calls a target. They have nothing in common. In UI Automation, a target represents the system under test.

Also, note how similar this syntax is to the way Apple retrieves singleton instances in Objective-C. Like [NSNotificationCenter defaultCenter], the localTarget() acts like a class method on what looks like a UIATarget class to retrieve this

---

1. http://developer.apple.com/library/ios/documentation/DeveloperTools/Reference/UIAutomationRef/_index.html

singleton. I say "acts like" because JavaScript's object model isn't quite the same as what we have in Objective-C. We'll get more into the features and quirks about that in Section 4.2, *Describing the App with Screen Objects*, on page 48.

Let's try to script deleting a search term from our list. We've already seen how the captured script drills down into the user interface on each line, but let's break up those long lines into something more manageable by using JavaScript variables:

02-Behavior/step01/remove_search_term.js
```
var target = UIATarget.localTarget();
var app = target.frontMostApp();
var window = app.mainWindow();
var tableView = window.tableViews()[0];
var cells = tableView.cells();
```

In JavaScript, we declare variables with the var keyword. The language is dynamically typed, so we don't specify the kind of data the variable can hold, and technically we don't even need to say var. But if we leave var off, then the variable is declared globally. To be safe, always practice declaring your JavaScript variables with var. Once we start using functions and objects to help organize our scripts, we'll want to ensure our variables are local. We don't want unintended side effects.

We ask the target for the frontmost application, ask that application for its main window, ask that window for the first table view, and then retrieve its cells. So, what is this list of cells and how do we find what we're looking for?

Searching through a UIAElementArray

When we ask for a collection of table cells, we get back a UIAElementArray. These act like JavaScript arrays but with a little bit of extra sugar on top.

At the simplest level, we can access the cells by indexing into the array with an integer, just like a normal JavaScript array. Here, we fetch the first cell:

02-Behavior/step01/remove_search_term.js
```
var firstCell = cells[0];
```

UIAElementArray provides several methods to search through the collection for what we want. For instance, withName() returns a new UIAElementArray with the results filtered to only elements with the given name:

02-Behavior/step01/remove_search_term.js
```
var filteredCells = cells.withName("coffee");
```

In our case, we only want the *first* cell with a given name. So, UI Automation provides firstWithName() to return the first one it finds. It's such a common operation that this method is also aliased to the [...] bracket syntax. To retrieve the table view cell with the search term "coffee," we simply have to do this:

02-Behavior/step01/remove_search_term.js
```
var coffeeCell = cells["coffee"];
```

We now have the cell named "coffee" in an instance variable ready to control. We want to expose the Delete button to write our acceptance test, so we'll need to learn a bit more about how these elements work.

Manipulating a UIAElement

Our object representing the table view is a kind of UIAElement. This base type provides common behavior for looking up subelements, checking for visibility, and manipulating with gestures and events. Each subtype targets more-specific behavior related to the different controls on the screen.

We've already seen this with the cells() method on the table view. This is a convenience method on the UIATableView subtype of UIAElement, which means we could query for all the children by calling elements(), but that would return the headers, footers, and all other elements inside the table view, not just the cells. Every element subtype has a nice set of these convenience methods that filter down the child elements to only those of the corresponding type.

If you think this all looks suspiciously similar to the UIView hierarchy, you're correct. UI Automation maps most of the UIView hierarchy onto these UIAElement objects. There's a UIAElement subtype for most of the standard views and controls in UIKit. Anything that the accessibility framework can see or traverse will show up in this element tree. We'll get into more detail about how the accessibility framework relates in Section 5.2, *Identifying Elements with Accessibility APIs*, on page 64.

Our table view follows the common editing convention where we can swipe to reveal a Delete button on a specific row, or we can turn on edit mode to show all the delete confirmation buttons. For simplicity's sake, let's turn on edit mode by tapping the Edit button in the navigation bar. Since we have the UIAWindow already saved in a variable, we could drill down to it from there, but since the navigation-bar concept is so central to normal iOS application layout, UI Automation includes a navigationBar() method on the application object itself. In fact, UIAApplication has a lot of helpers we can use to quickly access toolbars, tab bars, and even the keyboard. Let's grab the navigation bar, fetch the Edit button, and tap it like so:

```
02-Behavior/step02/remove_search_term.js
var navigationBar = app.navigationBar();
var editButton = navigationBar.leftButton();
if (editButton.name() == "Edit") {
    editButton.tap();
}

var coffeeCell = cells["coffee"];
```

We could have found the Edit button by searching through the buttons() element array for the first element with the name Edit, but since this is an instance of UIANavigationBar, we can use the convenience method to retrieve the button on the left side. Once we have the button, we're inspecting the button text to check whether the table is already in edit mode. If so, the button will say Done and we will continue. If not, we'll tap it to turn on edit mode. We're using this check here so we can run the script over and over while we're exploring. We're leaving the table in edit mode if it was there already.

Note that we need to tap the Edit button *before* we fetch the cell with the search term "coffee" from the table view. Turning on edit mode alters the table view in such a way that if we fetched the cell before turning on edit mode, we'd be holding on to an invalid element and not the one currently onscreen. Keep this in mind if the UIAElement objects you try to talk to seem out of sync with the user interface. It may be invalid, which would mean you need to fetch it again.

Exploring with logElementTree()

Now that we're in edit mode, we need to find the red delete-button toggle in the coffeeCell. The problem is that there's no text on it; it's just a red dash. We can find it with the logElementTree() method that every UIAElement supports. It prints the element hierarchy to the trace log right at the point it was called:

```
02-Behavior/step02/remove_search_term.js
coffeeCell.logElementTree();
```

Run the script with this line at the end; we'll see output similar to what the following figure shows.

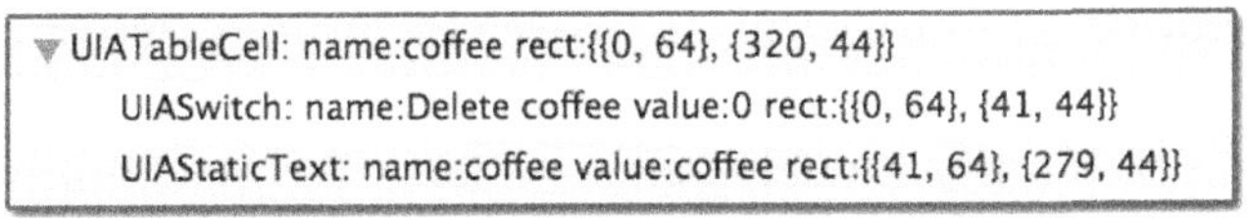

```
▼ UIATableCell: name:coffee rect:{{0, 64}, {320, 44}}
    UIASwitch: name:Delete coffee value:0 rect:{{0, 64}, {41, 44}}
    UIAStaticText: name:coffee value:coffee rect:{{41, 64}, {279, 44}}
```

Figure 13—Checking the hierarchy with logElementTree()

There's a UIASwitch named Delete coffee, followed by our UIAStaticText, which is the UILabel for coffee. Let's tap that switch and log the element tree again to see what happens next:

02-Behavior/step02/remove_search_term.js
```
var deleteSwitch = coffeeCell.switches()[0];
if (deleteSwitch.value() == 0) {
    deleteSwitch.tap();
}

coffeeCell.logElementTree();
```

We fetch the delete switch as the first (and only) switch in the cell. Then we check its value to see if it's already switched on. If it's off, we tap it. Just like the check for the table's edit mode, this lets us keep running the script even if the previous run left the switch on. After flipping the switch, the Delete button appears so we're logging the element tree again to find out what it is and how to tap it.

When run, the trace log shows output from the following figure. Notice how the switch's value is now set to 1, and we have a new button named *Confirm Deletion for coffee*. We could look up that button by name if we want. But since our cells are so simple and don't have any other buttons, we can simply tap the first one we see:

02-Behavior/step02/remove_search_term.js
```
var deleteButton = coffeeCell.buttons()[0];
deleteButton.tap();
```

```
▼ UIATableCell: name:coffee rect:{{0, 64}, {320, 44}}
    UIASwitch: name:Delete coffee value:1 rect:{{0, 64}, {41, 44}}
    UIAStaticText: name:coffee value:coffee rect:{{41, 64}, {204, 44}}
    UIAButton: name:Confirm Deletion for coffee rect:{{245, 64}, {75, 44}}
```

When we run this script, the "coffee" cell is removed from the list. We'll talk more about resetting the app data to a consistent state in Chapter 8, *Setting Up Application Data*, on page 121, but for the moment you'll need to remember to manually re-create the "coffee" search term in the list after each test run.

We have a great understanding of the basic objects and elements that make up the scripting interface. However, our tests aren't as useful if we can't make assertions and communicate failed expectations. We need our scripts to tell us when things go wrong, so let's talk a bit about the logging mechanism next.

2.2 Reporting Errors

UI Automation logs all its activity to the trace log. Up to this point Instruments has treated our log messages neutrally. We need some way to flag an error, both for the test-runner to know that something went wrong and so we can see the error when we go back over the logs.

Our acceptance test should fail if the table cell isn't deleted. To check for this, we can tell the automation-scripting interface to wait for the cell to become invalid:

```
02-Behavior/step03/remove_search_term.js
target.pushTimeout(0.1);
coffeeCell.waitForInvalid();
target.popTimeout();
```

The pushTimeout() and popTimeout() methods on the UIATarget are our way of telling the system how long to wait when querying the interface. By default, an unsuccessful query will time out after a couple of seconds. This is just in case an animation or other kind of transition is still running. Since we're confident that the cell shouldn't be there anymore, we can push a very short timeout, 0.1 second in this case, onto the timeout stack to force UI Automation to quickly return control to our script. We call the popTimeout() method to put the original timeout value back the way it was.

With the short timeout set, we call the waitForInvalid() method on the cell. This pauses the script—up to the timeout limit—for the element to possibly disappear from the screen. Once control returns to us, we check the element to see if it is gone by using the isValid() method:

```
02-Behavior/step03/remove_search_term.js
if (coffeeCell.isValid()) {
    UIALogger.logError("Oops. Cell is still there!");
} else {
    UIALogger.logMessage("Cell is gone, we're all set!");
}
```

Here we see UIALogger for the first time. This object provides several methods to flag log output with different states. In this case, we are using the UIALogger.logError() method to indicate something went wrong, and the UIALogger.logMessage() method to indicate that everything is fine. We'll dig more into the different log types in Section 3.4, *Grouping Test Steps and Their Output*, on page 32, but for now this is sufficient.

Before running this script, make sure there is a "coffee" search term in the list. To force this assertion to fail, let's change our table view controller so that it doesn't update the table view when the search term is deleted. Let's comment out these lines:

02-Behavior/step03/NearbyMe/NBMSearchViewController.m
```
NSManagedObjectContext *context =
    [self.fetchedResultsController managedObjectContext];
//[context deleteObject:
//    [self.fetchedResultsController objectAtIndexPath:indexPath]];
```

02-Behavior/step03/NearbyMe/NBMSearchViewController.m
```
case NSFetchedResultsChangeDelete:
    //[tableView deleteRowsAtIndexPaths:[NSArray arrayWithObject:indexPath]
    //              withRowAnimation:UITableViewRowAnimationFade];
    break;
```

Now when we choose Profile from the Product menu, Xcode will rebuild the project, install it in the simulator, and switch back to Instruments, ready for us to continue. If the app didn't launch automatically, click the red record button in the upper left of the Instruments window to start the trace and launch the app.

In the following figure, we see our message with the Error log type. When we click on the line we see the full error along with a screenshot of the app at that point in time. This is a great way to help unwind what happened when the behavior isn't right. We can backtrack through the trace log to find out what states the application went through to see exactly how it failed.

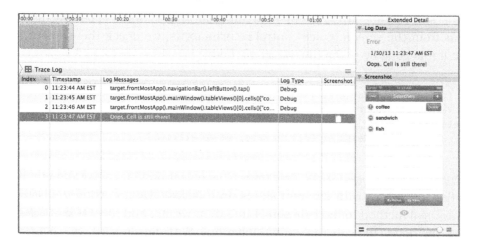

Figure 14—Oops; the cell is still there.

In the track pane, we also see a red region in the timeline for the UI Automation instrument track. This can be a quick way to scrub through the entire test run looking for failure points. If we click on any point in the timeline track, the trace log will select the line at that point in time and show more detail.

This is part of what makes UI Automation so unique among other testing options. The integration with Instruments gives you the ability to watch the application state change over time. We can add instruments for leak detection or CPU usage to our trace document, and when our automation tests run, we can browse back through the timeline to see exactly what the app was up to under the hood. We'll take advantage of this later, in Chapter 7, *Automating Performance Tests*, on page 101.

We're not done yet. We've only seen the test fail. Let's finish the job and watch it pass.

2.3 Verifying that the Test Does What It Says

Now that we know our test will fail properly if the app doesn't behave, let's finish by tidying up our script to make it easier for us to identify and verify what it's doing. Switch back to the script editor and add log messages to help explain each step as it happens:

```
02-Behavior/step04/remove_search_term.js
var target = UIATarget.localTarget();
var app = target.frontMostApp();
var window = app.mainWindow();
var tableView = window.tableViews()[0];
var cells = tableView.cells();

UIALogger.logMessage("Turn on edit mode");
var navigationBar = app.navigationBar();
var editButton = navigationBar.leftButton();
editButton.tap();

UIALogger.logMessage("Delete cell named 'coffee'");
var coffeeCell = cells["coffee"];

var deleteSwitch = coffeeCell.switches()[0];
deleteSwitch.tap();

var deleteButton = coffeeCell.buttons()[0];
deleteButton.tap();

target.pushTimeout(0.1);
coffeeCell.waitForInvalid();
target.popTimeout();
```

```
if (coffeeCell.isValid()) {
    UIALogger.logError("Oops. Cell is still there!");
} else {
    UIALogger.logMessage("Cell is gone, we're all set!");
}
```

➤ `UIALogger.logMessage("Turn off edit mode");`
➤ `editButton.tap();`

These log messages help break up the script into its discrete sections, like a comment for what the code is about to do. And because they are log messages, our intent is printed to our trace log in Instruments. If the test fails we can backtrack in the log and get even more useful hints for which behavior failed. How fine-grained should these log messages get? That's up to you and what you need to help you track down problems. These three log messages are sufficient for this test.

We're also adding one extra command at the very end. By tapping the Edit button after deleting the cell, we turn off edit mode on the table view. It's nice to clean up after ourselves when we're done.

Before we can run this test, we need to fix the bug we introduced. Switch back to Xcode and uncomment the following lines in the search table view controller to restore the behavior that deleted the search term:

02-Behavior/step04/NearbyMe/NBMSearchViewController.m
```
NSManagedObjectContext *context =
    [self.fetchedResultsController managedObjectContext];
[context deleteObject:
    [self.fetchedResultsController objectAtIndexPath:indexPath]];
```

02-Behavior/step04/NearbyMe/NBMSearchViewController.m
```
case NSFetchedResultsChangeDelete:
    [tableView deleteRowsAtIndexPaths:[NSArray arrayWithObject:indexPath]
                    withRowAnimation:UITableViewRowAnimationFade];
    break;
```

Remember to rebuild and profile the app again in Xcode once you make the changes so that the bug fix shows up in Instruments. To run the test, make sure that Run on Record is checked in the left sidebar and click the red record button at the top left of Instruments to stop and start a new trace recording.

The app launches and we see the progression in Figure 12, *Deleting the "coffee" search term*, on page 11. The table view goes into edit mode, the "coffee" cell asks for confirmation, the Delete button is tapped, the cell vanishes, and our script prints a success message to the trace log as in the following figure. Woot!

Index	⌃	Timestamp	Log Messages	Log Type	Screenshot
0		2:26:30 PM EST	Turn on edit mode	Default	
1		2:26:30 PM EST	target.frontMostApp().navigationBar().leftButton().tap()	Debug	
2		2:26:30 PM EST	Delete cell named 'coffee'	Default	
3		2:26:31 PM EST	target.frontMostApp().mainWindow().tableViews()[0].cells()["...	Debug	
4		2:26:32 PM EST	target.frontMostApp().mainWindow().tableViews()[0].cells()["...	Debug	
5		2:26:34 PM EST	Cell is gone, we're all set!	Default	
6		2:26:34 PM EST	Turn off edit mode	Default	
7		2:26:34 PM EST	target.frontMostApp().navigationBar().leftButton().tap()	Debug	

Figure 15—The final testing result

Throughout this chapter, we've seen the power that the integrated UI Automation instrument gives us. Granted, the script looks pretty long and verbose for such simple actions. It's cumbersome to manually embed a testing script every time we want to run our tests. This makes it hard to test many scenarios at once. And we haven't even discussed what to do to put apps in a consistent starting state!

We'll address these points soon. This chapter's goal was to get us used to writing our own scripts. UI Automation gives us lots of power to automate, capture, and trace what happens to our system under test. It's a great way for us to keep exploring the concepts and techniques behind testing through the user interface.

In the next chapter we'll write more acceptance tests and start building a master script to run all of them at once. We'll expand on our basic automation knowledge and experiment with testing more-complicated scenarios, like handling alert views and putting the search term we deleted back in the list.

CHAPTER 3

Building a Test Suite

We've learned the basics of UI Automation and written our first test. We're ready to keep going and test more behaviors of our app, but where do we put these new tests? We could keep appending snippets to form one long embedded test script, but this will get complicated quickly. It's time to think about new ways to structure our tests. We're going to start building up a *test suite* composed of self-contained scripts.

There are three goals to keep in mind. First, we want a way to separate and organize our scripts into text files that make managing and editing them easier. Second, we want a single master script that runs all our individual test scripts at once. And third, we need a way to organize the output of all these tests, bundling the details together, to reduce clutter so we can quickly find success and failure messages.

We're going to explore how to achieve these goals while writing two more acceptance tests for our app. These tests will expose us to some new automation concepts, like how to handle modal alert views and how to check results fetched over a network. By the end, we'll have a master script that runs our three tests in sequence to verify three important behaviors of our app. Let's get started!

3.1 Testing with a Modal Alert View

Practicality is a great guide when choosing which test to write next. Since we're expecting these tests to execute sequentially, it makes sense to undo the change we made in the first test we wrote, back in Chapter 2, *Testing Behavior with UI Automation*, on page 11. We removed the search term "coffee"; let's put it back. This not only tests the behavior a user will normally want to perform, but also puts the application back in a consistent state and ready for the next test in our sequence.

When we first attempted to capture our actions back in *Limitations of Capturing Actions*, on page 8, tapping the + button to add a search term popped up an alert view with a focused text field showing the keyboard. UI Automation couldn't capture interactions with the alert view and left a comment for us to do it ourselves. Well, now is our chance to learn how.

First, make sure the application is built and ready to go in Instruments, like we first did in Section 2.1, *Talking to the UI through JavaScript*, on page 12. Once Instruments is loaded up with UI Automation, create a new script in the trace document just like we did in Figure 4, *Choosing to create a script*, on page 4.

Since we're starting with a blank slate, we'll need the familiar setup. Grab the root user-interface elements and store them in variables at the top of our script:

03-BuildingTestSuite/step01/add_search_term.js
```
var target = UIATarget.localTarget();
var app = target.frontMostApp();
var window = app.mainWindow();
```

To add a search term, we need to tap the + button in the navigation bar to trigger the alert:

03-BuildingTestSuite/step01/add_search_term.js
```
UIALogger.logMessage("Adding search term 'coffee'");

app.navigationBar().rightButton().tap();
app.keyboard().typeString("coffee");
```

We print a log message describing what the next set of actions is attempting to do. We dig down into the UIANavigationBar element of the UIAApplication, find the button on the right side, and tap it. We then ask the UIAApplication for the keyboard and tell it to type in the string "coffee."

At first glance, this makes sense. We expect our script to run all the way through and type into the keyboard. Let's try it and see what happens. The app runs, the alert shows up asking the user to type in a search term, but then it is immediately canceled before the our script attempts to type. To diagnose the problem, let's examine the error message in Figure 16, *The keyboard is missing*, on page 25.

The UIAKeyboard element was unable to tap the c key. By looking at the debug messages in the trace log, we can try to figure out what happened. The right navigation-bar button was tapped, and we see the command telling the keyboard to type the string, but the third debug line is puzzling. It looks like the

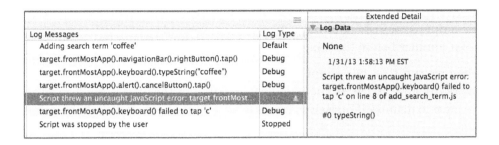

Log Messages	Log Type	Extended Detail
		▼ Log Data
Adding search term 'coffee'	Default	None
target.frontMostApp().navigationBar().rightButton().tap()	Debug	1/31/13 1:58:13 PM EST
target.frontMostApp().keyboard().typeString("coffee")	Debug	Script threw an uncaught JavaScript error:
target.frontMostApp().alert().cancelButton().tap()	Debug	target.frontMostApp().keyboard() failed to
Script threw an uncaught JavaScript error: target.frontMost...	⚠	tap 'c' on line 8 of add_search_term.js
target.frontMostApp().keyboard() failed to tap 'c'	Debug	#0 typeString()
Script was stopped by the user	Stopped	

Figure 16—The keyboard is missing.

alert view was canceled before the keyboard element tried to tap out the string. We never attempted to tap the cancelButton() on the alert in our script. Why is it here in the log?

Because alerts are system-wide modal views, they suspend user interaction to the rest of the app. Following this pattern, UI Automation pauses the normal script flow until the alert is dismissed. By default, the scripting engine will dismiss alerts immediately with whatever is marked as the cancel button.

We need to change this behavior by giving the scripting engine a function that will be called when alerts pop up. This kind of pattern is similar to the way callback blocks work in Objective-C and *event handlers* work in JavaScript.

Let's set up our custom event handler by assigning a function to the UIATarget object's onAlert property:

```
03-BuildingTestSuite/step02/add_search_term.js
UIATarget.onAlert = function() {
    return true;
};

app.navigationBar().rightButton().tap();
app.keyboard().typeString("coffee");
```

This is the simplest onAlert handler we could write. By returning true, we are saying that *we* want to handle the alert and dismiss it ourselves. The alert will remain on the screen, and as soon as the onAlert handler returns, control will resume in the main body of our script.

By contrast, returning false tells the scripting engine to do what it normally does: tap the cancel button. This is a great way to "fall through" to the default behavior if we decide that we don't need to do anything special in our handler.

Make sure this is *above* the script line that taps the + button. Remember, our script pauses when the alert shows up, so we need to establish our custom onAlert handler before that happens.

When we run this, our script doesn't fail with an error like before. The alert shows up, and "coffee" is successfully typed in, but the alert doesn't go away. We have to dismiss it ourselves because we told the system we're taking care of it:

03-BuildingTestSuite/step03/add_search_term.js
```
UIATarget.onAlert = function() {
    return true;
};

app.navigationBar().rightButton().tap();
app.keyboard().typeString("coffee");
app.alert().defaultButton().tap();
```

We're asking the UIAApplication for the visible alert, asking the alert for its default button, and then tapping it.

To review, we set up the alert handler first and then tap the + button in the navigation bar. Our script blocks while the alert handler is called. We simply return true to tell the system that we will handle it ourselves. Control returns to the main body of our script, where we then type the string "coffee," and finally we find the visible alert and tap the default button, confirming our new search term and adding it to the list.

Alert handlers can be far more robust than we've touched on here. Our use case is so simple that this is a great way to get to know how they work and interrupt our normal script flow. We'll cover more-advanced uses in Section 5.4, *Advanced Alert-Handling*, on page 72.

Now that the alert handler is set up, our script won't block and we can write our assertion. The app is supposed to add new search terms to the top of the list. To test this, we grab the first cell in the table view and check its name:

03-BuildingTestSuite/step04/add_search_term.js
```
var cell = window.tableViews()[0].cells()[0];
if (cell.name() == "coffee") {
    UIALogger.logMessage("'coffee' search term is there");
} else {
    UIALogger.logError("Expected 'coffee' but got '" + cell.name() + "'");
}
```

If it's the one we created, say so; otherwise flag it as an error so it shows up red in the trace log.

We have two tests—one to remove a search term named "coffee" and one to re-create it. Next we'll discuss how to run them back-to-back by loading them from the file system on the fly.

3.2 Importing Script Files at Runtime

At the moment, we have two individual tests that we want to run one after the other. Embedding scripts in UI Automation's editor is useful and convenient, but it's not the best way to maintain our test scripts long-term. Instead we will have the Instruments trace document reference a master script on the file system. This script can then import other script files at runtime. Using these techniques, we'll be able to run both our tests in the right order and still keep them separate.

Let's construct this master script in place and then export it to a file. Create a blank script in the automation-script editor and type in these #import statements to tell the scripting engine that we want to pull other files into this script:

```
03-BuildingTestSuite/step05/test_suite.js
#import "remove_search_term.js"
#import "add_search_term.js"
```

The #import statement is not official JavaScript. It's unique to UI Automation, which interprets it as a command to evaluate and insert the imported file into the current script, similar to the way the #import preprocessor statement works in Objective-C. The contents are imported and evaluated only once for each imported file. Even if you import two separate files that both try to import a third file, the third file is imported only once. We'll go over more details and edge cases regarding the #import statement when we get to advanced test-organization techniques in Chapter 4, *Organizing Test Code*, on page 41.

Importing script files like this doesn't work for embedded scripts in trace documents like we've been writing so far. The runtime tries to find script files relative to the current directory, but there isn't a current directory for an embedded script. We need to first *export* this master script to the file system. Control-click or right-click anywhere in the script pane and choose Export from the pop-up context menu. Save it in the root of the project with the file name test_suite.js. Do the same thing with the other two test scripts we've been writing, and name them remove_search_term.js and add_search_term.js, respectively.

Now we see our scripts show up by name in the left-hand sidebar of the UI Automation instrument, like in the following figure. They are no longer embedded scripts. The Instruments trace document maintains links to the files in the file system. Whichever script is selected in the sidebar will be the one that runs.

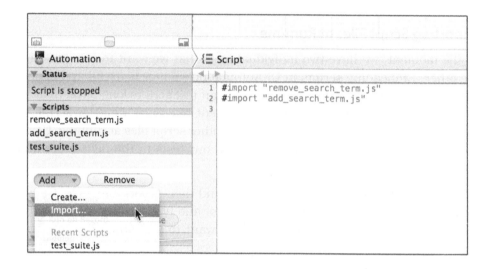

Figure 17—Referencing external scripts into the trace document

Before we try out our test suite, we'll make sure the application starts in the proper state with a "coffee" search term at the top of the list. When run, our master script instructs UI Automation to import the first test and run it, and then tells UI Automation to import and run the second test. We have a test suite!

Importing like this makes it a bit easier to edit test scripts. Although the UI Automation script editor provides syntax highlighting and error annotations, it's not much more robust than that. By importing a script file, we can edit in an external text editor, like BBEdit or vi, and when we switch back to UI Automation, it asks if it should reload the file. Changes made in UI Automation will immediately save to the script file so they show up in the external editor.

Breaking scripts up like this also lets us divide and conquer the test suite. If you want to run a single test over and over while you're working on it, import that script file into the trace document by choosing Add > Import from the left sidebar, as in Figure 17, *Referencing external scripts into the trace document*, on page 28, and select it to run it by itself. When you're ready to run the whole suite, import and select the master test_suite.js file, make sure the application is in the proper starting state, and run everything together.

3.3 Testing Results from a Live API

Let's keep the momentum going and write our third acceptance test to add to this suite. We'll build it separately from the others and iterate on it until we get it right, and then we'll use the #import statement to pull it in when we run our master script.

The app is supposed to fetch results from OpenStreetMap for the selected search term within the visible map area. We'll test the map itself later, in Chapter 5, *Maps, Gestures, and Alerts*, on page 59. For the moment, we just want to test that we get *something* back that represents success, and we can do that by inspecting the results table view.

First, make sure the application starts in the right state. Launch the app in the simulator through Xcode and check that the "coffee" search term is somewhere in the list. Also, we need to make sure the app has permission to access the location services.

If you haven't already done so on your own, tap on the "coffee" search term yourself and then confirm the location-permissions alert. We'll go into more detail about dealing with this alert automatically and choosing a location when testing in the simulator in Section 9.1, *Choosing a Geographical Location*, on page 147, but for now this is sufficient.

Profile the application in Instruments, create a new embedded script, right-click in the script editor, and export it to the root of the project in a file named check_results_list.js. Type in the familiar set of variable declarations at the top:

03-BuildingTestSuite/step06/check_results_list.js
```
var target = UIATarget.localTarget();
var app = target.frontMostApp();
var window = app.mainWindow();
```

To get to the search results, we need to tap a search term:

03-BuildingTestSuite/step06/check_results_list.js
```
UIALogger.logMessage("Tapping 'coffee'");

var tableView = window.tableViews()[0];
tableView.cells()["coffee"].tap();
```

We ask the window for its first UIATableView and then we search for any cell with the name "coffee" and tap it. This brings us to the results view controller that shows the map by default. We want to switch to the list representation, so let's find the button to trigger it:

```
03-BuildingTestSuite/step06/check_results_list.js
UIALogger.logMessage("Switching to list of results");

var toolbar = app.toolbar();
var resultsSwitcher = toolbar.segmentedControls()[0];

resultsSwitcher.buttons()["List"].tap();
```

We're asking the UIAApplication object for its global UIAToolbar instance. Then we search for the first segmented control and keep track of that in a variable. We look up the first button in that control with the name List, and tap it.

Now we can hunt for a search result to make sure we're getting the correct data back, but we have two things to worry about. First, we're now looking at *a different table view than the one we interacted with earlier*. We saved the UIATableView representing the search terms in the tableView variable earlier, but that element is no longer on the screen. We need to find the *current* table view representing the list of results on the screen.

Second, the OpenStreetMap API could return different results by the time you run this test. That's one of the challenges of testing applications that integrate with external dependencies we cannot control. We'll dig into stubbing those out in Chapter 9, *Stubbing External Services*, on page 147, but for the moment we may need to adjust the assertion of this test to match the data coming back.

With these two issues in mind, let's grab the new table view and fetch a cell with the name of a search result we expect:

```
03-BuildingTestSuite/step06/check_results_list.js
var expected = "Coffee Cabin, 0.6 mi";
UIALogger.logMessage("Checking for '" + expected + "'");

// Fetch the *new* table view of results
var tableView = window.tableViews()[0];
var cell = tableView.cells()[expected];
```

We're using UIALogger.logMessage() to provide a checkpoint in the midst of our test. Since we're trying to identify a specific point of interest that is tied to an external API that we can't control, it's helpful to see in the trace log what we are attempting to do. We then look up the new table view in the window and try to find one of its cells with the expected name.

The cell name includes the content of both the main label with the name of the point of interest, and the detail label with the distance from the current location. UITableViewCell instances give us this convenience by default. They expose a combination of the text labels as the UIATableCell element's name. We'll discuss how this works when we talk about the accessibility API in Section 5.2, *Identifying Elements with Accessibility APIs*, on page 64, but keep this in mind for now as you pick a point of interest that satisfies this test.

When we asked the UIATableView element for a cell with the expected name, we got *something* back, but what if the element we were looking for wasn't found? In that case, we get back a UIAElementNil object. These nil elements are useful because they act like stand-ins for real elements. Nil elements are always invalid, so we can check whether our query was successful by using the isValid() method:

03-BuildingTestSuite/step06/check_results_list.js
```
if (cell.isValid()) {
    UIALogger.logMessage("Found '" + expected + "'");
} else {
    UIALogger.logError("Expected search result '" + expected + "'");
}
```

If the cell represents a real table cell on the screen, then the isValid() method returns true and we say so in the log. Otherwise, we log this as an error and continue.

Our test is technically done, but we should clean up after ourselves by tapping the Back button:

03-BuildingTestSuite/step06/check_results_list.js
```
window.navigationBar().leftButton().tap();
```

We're executing the entire test suite within a single run of the application because resetting the application to a known state is a more advanced topic. We'll go into more detail about resetting the environment and executing tests in isolation in Chapter 10, *Command-Line Workflow*, on page 165. For now, we need to take these extra steps to make sure our tests play nicely together.

On that note, let's import this test file into our suite:

03-BuildingTestSuite/step06/test_suite.js
```
#import "remove_search_term.js"
#import "add_search_term.js"
➤ #import "check_results_list.js"
```

Running the test suite exercises all the behaviors at once: a search term is removed, it is put back, and then we check to make sure a result comes back from OpenStreetMap.

We've started organizing our scripts by breaking them out into separate files and importing them, and we've successfully stitched together the beginnings of our test suite using a master script. Next we're going to learn how to organize the test output so we can distinguish the results in the trace log. Let's look deeper into logging with UI Automation.

3.4 Grouping Test Steps and Their Output

Our test suite is three behavioral tests strong, and we now have a lot of output to wade through in the trace log. The figure here shows what a successful run through the whole suite generates.

Log Messages	Log Type
Turn on edit mode	Default
target.frontMostApp().navigationBar().leftButton().tap()	Debug
Delete cell named 'coffee'	Default
target.frontMostApp().mainWindow().tableViews()[0].cells()["coffee"].switches()[0].tap()	Debug
target.frontMostApp().mainWindow().tableViews()[0].cells()["coffee"].buttons()[0].tap()	Debug
Cell is gone, we're all set!	Default
Turn off edit mode	Default
target.frontMostApp().navigationBar().leftButton().tap()	Debug
Adding search term 'coffee'	Default
target.frontMostApp().navigationBar().rightButton().tap()	Debug
target.frontMostApp().keyboard().typeString("coffee")	Debug
target.frontMostApp().alert().defaultButton().tap()	Debug
'coffee' search term is there	Default
Tapping 'coffee'	Default
target.frontMostApp().mainWindow().tableViews()[0].cells()["coffee"].tap()	Debug
Switching to list of results	Default
target.frontMostApp().toolbar().segmentedControls()[0].buttons()["List"].tap()	Debug
Checking for 'Coffee Cabin, 0.6 mi'	Default
Found 'Coffee Cabin, 0.6 mi'	Default
target.frontMostApp().mainWindow().navigationBar().leftButton().tap()	Debug

Figure 18—A mess of log lines

It's difficult to know where one test ends and the other begins. It's not impossible to read, but we don't have to settle for this; UI Automation provides even more options for logging. We're going to cover log groups and organize the suite output to make it easier to see the behavior boundaries.

UIALogger provides methods that act like markers to roll up log messages into a single collapsed group in the trace log. Let's see this in action by focusing on the test we just wrote, which checks the table view of results. Click check_results_list.js in the UI Automation script sidebar, switch to the script editor pane, and add these two lines at the top and bottom of the file:

03-BuildingTestSuite/step07/check_results_list.js

```
➤ UIALogger.logStart("Testing results lists for 'coffee'");

  var target = UIATarget.localTarget();
  var app = target.frontMostApp();
  var window = app.mainWindow();

  // ...

  window.navigationBar().leftButton().tap();

➤ UIALogger.logPass("Test complete");
```

The UIALogger.logStart() method begins a log group with the name that we pass in. All the subsequent log output will now be grouped under this name until either a new group is opened with another call to logStart(), or we explicitly close the group like we do here with logPass(). Log groups are only one level deep. Trying to open another group will start a new one rather than nest.

When we run this test we have a single line in our trace log, with a disclosure triangle at the beginning. Expanding the log group shows the messages inside. Our test output is grouped with the Pass log type and all the details are tucked away unless we want to see them, as in the following figure.

Log Messages	Log Type
▼ Testing results lists for 'coffee'	Pass
Tapping 'coffee'	Default
target.frontMostApp().mainWindow().tableViews()[0].cells()["coffee"].tap()	Debug
Switching to list of results	Default
target.frontMostApp().toolbar().segmentedControls()[0].buttons()["List"].tap()	Debug
Checking for 'Coffee Cabin, 0.6 mi"	Default
Found 'Coffee Cabin, 0.6 mi'	Default
target.frontMostApp().mainWindow().navigationBar().leftButton().tap()	Debug
Test complete	Pass

Figure 19—Messages tucked away in a log group

Let's experiment and see what it looks like when the test fails. Change the line where we specify the expected search term name, and put something unexpected in there instead:

03-BuildingTestSuite/step08/check_results_list.js

```
var expected = "Unexpected Result";
UIALogger.logMessage("Checking for '" + expected + '"');

// Fetch the *new* table view of results
var tableView = window.tableViews()[0];
var cell = tableView.cells()[expected];
```

Now when we run our test, the log group is flagged as an error. But if we click the disclosure triangle, we'll see the passing log message at the very end of the group, as in the following figure.

Log Messages	Log Type
▼ Testing results lists for 'coffee'	Error
Tapping 'coffee'	Default
target.frontMostApp().mainWindow().tableViews()[0].cells()["coffee"].tap()	Debug
Switching to list of results	Default
target.frontMostApp().toolbar().segmentedControls()[0].buttons()["List"].tap()	Debug
Checking for 'Unexpected Result"	Default
Expected search result 'Unexpected Result'	Error
target.frontMostApp().mainWindow().navigationBar().leftButton().tap()	Debug
Test complete	Pass

Figure 20—Showing a passing log message

The log group itself takes on the most severe message type that it contains, which is why the whole group is marked as an error. But since we're just blindly calling UIALogger.logPass() at the end, we have a somewhat confusing message closing out the group. Instead, we should use logFail() to close out the log group with a failure type.

In our example here, we are making only one assertion, so we could close the log group right after logging the error. However, when we need to make more than one assertion in a test, which is common due to the complexity of user interfaces, we will need a way to interrupt our test and jump to the end to close the log group. That's where JavaScript exceptions come in handy.

Exceptional Logging

We can leverage JavaScript's exception handling to interrupt the normal flow of the script, calling logFail() instead of logPass() when an assertion fails. Don't worry—unlike in Objective-C, exceptions in JavaScript are quite safe and don't mess things up in memory.

Let's try this out by wrapping the test in a try/catch block and throwing an Error object instead of calling logError() directly:

```
03-BuildingTestSuite/step09/check_results_list.js
try {
    UIALogger.logStart("Testing results lists for 'coffee'");

    // ...

    if (!cell.isValid()) {
        throw new Error("Expected search result '" + expected + "'");
    }

    window.navigationBar().leftButton().tap();

    UIALogger.logPass("Test passed");
} catch(exception) {
}
```

Any time we pass an object to the throw keyword, the script immediately jumps into the catch block with that thrown object as the argument. Once we handle the exception, the script execution continues after the catch block. Technically, you can throw anything you want, but because of the way the UI Automation runtime works, throwing Error objects provides extra metadata, such as the line number and file where the exception occurred.

Of course, we need to do something with the exception once it is caught. Here's where we can log the error and close the log group:

```
03-BuildingTestSuite/step09/check_results_list.js
} catch(exception) {
    UIALogger.logError(exception.message);
    UIATarget.localTarget().logElementTree();
    UIALogger.logFail("Test failed");
}
```

We're passing the value of the message property on the Error object to UIALogger.logError(). Then we're telling the local target to log its element tree as a convenience. This will provide even more UI state information to compare when we're looking for problems. And finally, we close the log group with a failure message (see Figure 21, *Closing the log group as a failure*, on page 36).

Our test should still be failing because of the change we made earlier, so let's run this again and see what happens in the trace log.

Now we see the log group close as a failure and the dump of the element tree is right there after the error message. Let's fix our test so it checks for a proper result, as shown in the following code:

Log Messages	Log Type
▼ Testing results lists for 'coffee'	Fail
Tapping 'coffee'	Default
target.frontMostApp().mainWindow().tableViews()[0].cells()["coffee"].tap()	Debug
Switching to list of results	Default
target.frontMostApp().toolbar().segmentedControls()[0].buttons()["List"].tap()	Debug
Checking for 'Unexpected Result'	Default
Expected search result 'Unexpected Result'	Error
▶ UIATarget: name:iPhone Simulator rect:{{0, 0}, {320, 480}}	Debug
Test failed	Fail

Figure 21—Closing the log group as a failure

03-BuildingTestSuite/step10/check_results_list.js
```
var expected = "Coffee Cabin, 0.6 mi";
UIALogger.logMessage("Checking for '" + expected + "'");

// Fetch the *new* table view of results
var tableView = window.tableViews()[0];
var cell = tableView.cells()[expected];
```

Our test is in a working state now, but we have one more tweak to make to our exception handler to ensure we don't throw away script errors. To demonstrate, let's cause a runtime error by calling a nonexistent function at the start of the try block:

03-BuildingTestSuite/step11/check_results_list.js
```
try {
    UIALogger.logStart("Testing results lists for 'coffee'");

    foo();      // Trying to cause a script error with a bad function

    // ...
```

If we try to run this, our exception handler catches the runtime script error and we log the error message, but we lose the extra information, such as the line number and filename, that helps us debug what went wrong. To solve this, let's rethrow the Error object so that the script runtime can handle it, too.

03-BuildingTestSuite/step12/check_results_list.js
```
} catch(exception) {
    UIALogger.logError(exception.message);
    UIATarget.localTarget().logElementTree();
    UIALogger.logFail("Test failed");
    throw exception;
}
```

When we run with this more robust exception handler, our Error object bubbles up to the trace log, as the following figure shows. If we switch over to the script pane to view the problem, the line with the error is highlighted and annotated as it should be.

Figure 22—Ensuring we don't swallow and hide runtime script errors

We get several benefits from rethrowing the exception. When it reaches the scripting engine, it prints out the line number where it was thrown and annotates the script in the editor pane, making it easier to find out where the problem happened. UI Automation will also list the stack trace in the details sidebar on the right once we start using JavaScript functions to reuse test code.

Rethrowing the exception effectively aborts the whole script, but that is a good thing in our case since these tests depend on each other leaving the application in a certain state, like steps in a narrative. We're removing, then adding, then searching, and if an error interrupts a test group, it's possible that the application won't be in the proper state for the next test in the sequence to start. For the tests we're going to write here, aborting at the first sign of failure gives us a chance to fix things before we try again.

Grouping the Output of Our Other Two Tests

Now that we're implementing log groups with robust exception handling, let's port this paradigm to the other two tests in our suite. First let's do the test to remove the search term:

```
03-BuildingTestSuite/step13/remove_search_term.js
try {
    UIALogger.logStart("Removing the 'coffee' search term");

    // ...

    if (coffeeCell.isValid()) {
        throw new Error("Oops. Cell is still there!");
    }
```

```
    UIALogger.logMessage("Turn off edit mode");
    editButton.tap();

    UIALogger.logPass("Test passed");
} catch(exception) {
    UIALogger.logError(exception.message);
    UIATarget.localTarget().logElementTree();
    UIALogger.logFail("Test failed");
    throw exception;
}
```

Other than wrapping it in our try/catch code, we only needed to change the assertion to throw an Error object instead of calling UIALogger.logError(). Next let's do the test to add a search term:

03-BuildingTestSuite/step13/add_search_term.js
```
try {
    UIALogger.logStart("Putting the 'coffee' term back in the list");

    // ...

➤   if (cell.name() != "coffee") {
➤       throw new Error("Expected 'coffee' but got '" + cell.name() + "'");
➤   }

    UIALogger.logPass("Test passed");
} catch(exception) {
    UIALogger.logError(exception.message);
    UIATarget.localTarget().logElementTree();
    UIALogger.logFail("Test failed");
    throw exception;
}
```

We're changing the assertion to throw the Error object if the cell isn't named "coffee." The rest is the same, just nestled in the exception handler.

Before we continue, fix the check_results_list.js script so that it works properly by removing the call to the nonexistent foo() method. Also, make sure the application is in the proper starting state with a "coffee" search term in the list.

When we run the whole test suite, we're greeted with passing test groups like we see in Figure 23, *Passing test suite*, on page 39. All of our test steps work together to remove, re-add, and do a cursory check of the search results. Running this suite raises our confidence that key features aren't broken.

UIALogger gives us a flexible mechanism to trigger log messages any way we want. These message types are like building blocks for annotating the test output to give us more information. We'll use additional message types later, but this is enough for now.

Log Messages	Log Type
▶ Removing the 'coffee' search term	Pass
▼ Putting the 'coffee' term back in the list	Pass
Adding search term 'coffee'	Default
target.frontMostApp().navigationBar().rightButton().tap()	Debug
target.frontMostApp().keyboard().typeString("coffee")	Debug
target.frontMostApp().alert().defaultButton().tap()	Debug
Test passed	Pass
▶ Testing results lists for 'coffee'	Pass

Figure 23—Passing test suite

We've come a long way and have quite a set of techniques to test behaviors in iOS apps. You could put down the book at this point and do quite well, but there's a whole lot more we can cover to make your testing more productive. In the next chapter we'll explore new opportunities to organize and reuse test code, and see how to leverage JavaScript for greater test readability.

CHAPTER 4

Organizing Test Code

One of the greatest challenges we face in automated UI testing is the brittle coupling between our test code and the app's interface. For example, if we have to move a button out of one superview and into another, or if the name of the button changes, then our tests will break. If we have to push that button in ten separate test scenarios, then we have ten places to update. This is what we mean when we say brittle; changes in the UI cause catastrophic changes in our tests. We can't always avoid writing brittle tests, but we can take steps to minimize the damage.

Another challenge is the line noise from the verbose scripting interface of UI Automation. Walking down the element tree to interact with the UI takes a lot of steps. For very complicated tests, the meaning of the test itself can be lost among the low-level implementation to achieve the scenario.

To fight back against these challenges, we're going to build a reusable toolbox extracted from the test code we've been writing for NearbyMe. We'll stay organized by writing our tests from the user's perspective. Test steps written at a high level hide the noise of actually finding and tapping elements. This gives us a vocabulary to write easily readable tests, helping us think clearly about the system as a whole and confirming at a glance that we are testing what we claim to be.

4.1 Starting a JavaScript Toolbox

As we've been writing the test code, we've seen some common patterns. For each of the three test scripts, we're writing a lot of boilerplate JavaScript code to set up, assert, and log the output. If we take some time to consider what we've done and extract the common parts to a reusable test environment, we can import that environment everywhere we need it, like a handy toolbox.

We'll think through three specific cases where we can simplify the verbose syntax of UI Automation. Each of these functions will be declared globally and available everywhere. We shouldn't do that lightly since we want to keep the global namespace free of cruft, but the convenience is compelling. We'll look at some of the reasoning behind each of these functions so you can evaluate if they make sense for testing your apps, and how you might grow your own tools to suit a unique context.

Setting Up a Test Environment in Strict Mode

Now that we're diving deeper into JavaScript, we should turn on *strict mode*. It protects us from silly mistakes that lead to confusing and hard-to-debug results. It's not as robust as a compiler, but it can catch many common errors for us and it's a great safety net while we're learning.

Create a directory named automation where we will put all of our UI Automation scripts from now on. This will help us be better organized and not fill the project's root directory. Create a file named automation/env.js, which will be our test environment. Open the NearbyMe project and begin profiling it with Instruments like we did in Section 1.1, *Capturing Our First Script from the Simulator*, on page 2. Choose the UI Automation template, and then import that env.js file into the script editor like we did in Section 3.2, *Importing Script Files at Runtime*, on page 27.

To turn on strict mode, we add a single line at the top of the file:

04-OrganizingTestCode/step01/automation/env.js
```
"use strict";
```

That line, with the string value "use strict", is the flag to the interpreter that we want the whole file to be in strict mode. Every file that you want in strict mode needs to have this line at the top.

Let's see strict mode in action by leaking a variable in a function to the global scope:

04-OrganizingTestCode/step01/automation/env.js
```
function polluteGlobalScope() {
    leaked = "test";     // NOT local variable
}

polluteGlobalScope();

UIALogger.logMessage(leaked);  // Outputs "test"
```

In JavaScript, any variable that's not declared with the var keyword in the local scope is assumed to be global. This often leads to accidentally sharing state between functions, and is one of the sneakiest sources of bugs for JavaScript beginners. If you really want a global variable, declare it first outside in the global scope with the var keyword; then it'll be visible in all other functions.

With strict mode enabled, running this script will show the error in the following figure. This gives us a similar, if limited, kind of confidence to the sort the Objective-C compiler gives us. You can scope strict mode to smaller pieces, like inside specific functions, but for this book we'll use it everywhere. For more details about strict mode, check out Mozilla's documentation.[1]

```
1  "use strict";
2
3  function polluteGlobalScope() {
4      leaked = "test";     // NOT local variable        Strict mode forbids implicit creation of global property 'leaked'
5  }
6
7  polluteGlobalScope();
8
9  UIALogger.logMessage(leaked);   // Outputs "test"
10
```

Figure 24—Strict mode requires the var keyword for variables.

We now have an env.js file flagged to run in strict mode. Our script environment is ready, so let's start populating it with our tools.

Painless Output with a log() Function

Our first tool candidate is a general-purpose logging function. Recall that we use UIALogger.logMessage() to output to the trace log a neutral message that doesn't get treated as an error condition. When a test fails or a scripting error occurs, we want to give ourselves plenty of hints that help us discover the application state leading up to the failure or error.

The name UIALogger is a pain to type every time, and interpolating variables in JavaScript gets longwinded. There's just too much friction to write something like this regularly:

```
var name1 = "coffee";
var name2 = "fish";
UIALogger.logMessage("We should see: " + name1 + ", " + name2);
```

Let's shorten this by using a tritely named JavaScript function. Since logging is going to be such a common operation, we'll name it log():

---

1. https://developer.mozilla.org/en-US/docs/JavaScript/Reference/Functions_and_function_scope/Strict_mode

04-OrganizingTestCode/step02/automation/env.js
```
function log(message) {
    UIALogger.logMessage(message);
}
```

This declares the function log() with a single argument. We're building the simplest wrapper around UIALogger.logMessage() so we can pass the string message through. This shortens our code, like so:

04-OrganizingTestCode/step02/automation/env.js
```
var name1 = "coffee";
var name2 = "fish";
log("We should see: " + name1 + ", " + name2);
```

Much better, but we're still doing our own string concatenation when we pass the message in. Instead we can leverage JavaScript's *variadic function* behavior to concatenate all the arguments we pass in:

04-OrganizingTestCode/step03/automation/env.js
```
function log() {     // Variable # of arguments
    var msg = Array.prototype.join.call(arguments, ', ');
    UIALogger.logMessage(msg);
}
```

A variadic function's argument list can be figured out at runtime. To make it clear in the code, I like to include an inline comment to explain the empty parameter list. Here we're using a little bit of JavaScript magic to combine all the arguments in one big comma-separated string. The arguments variable is available in all JavaScript functions and almost acts like an array holding all the arguments passed in. I say it *almost* acts like an array because for legacy reasons it lacks some basic array methods—like join(), in this case.

To combine all the arguments as a string, we can grab the join() method off the *prototype* of Array and call it as if it were bound to the arguments object. We'll go into a bit more detail about the JavaScript object model and prototypes in Section 4.3, *Reusing a Generic Screen Prototype*, on page 52, but for now know this works as if the arguments list had that method on it to begin with. Once the log() function is written, we are able to call it, like so:

04-OrganizingTestCode/step03/automation/env.js
```
var name1 = "coffee";
var name2 = "fish";
log("We should see", name1, name2);
```

Much better! As a bonus, any argument we pass in will be coerced to a string automatically because of the way join() works. We can efficiently express our thought process in these tests by reducing the friction for such a common operation as logging output.

Wrapping Log Groups in a test() Function

Up to this point, our tests have been made of simple assertions using if statements wrapped by log groups. Back in *Exceptional Logging*, on page 34, we wrapped each of our tests' steps in try/catch blocks and threw exceptions when an assertion failed so that we could close the log group as a failure and end the test:

```
try {
    UIALogger.logStart("Begin this test");

    //..
    if (somethingIsntRight) {
        throw new Error("Something isn't right");
    }
    UIALogger.logPass("Test passed");
} catch(exception) {
    UIALogger.logError(exception.message);
    UIATarget.localTarget().logElementTree();
    UIALogger.logFail("Test failed");
    throw exception;
}
```

It's a good way to short-circuit code when there's a problem, but this is pretty verbose syntactical ceremony to write out every time we want to group-test output. We can do better by wrapping it all in a single function for reuse:

04-OrganizingTestCode/step04/automation/env.js
```
test("Test throwing a string", function() {
    throw new Error("This is an error");
});
```

This is a much cleaner way to mark a batch of test steps. We call this by passing in a string to describe the log group and passing in an *anonymous function* as the second parameter that contains our test steps. Our test() function calls our steps in the try/catch block for us, like so:

04-OrganizingTestCode/step04/automation/env.js
```
function test(description, steps) {
    try {
        UIALogger.logStart(description);
        steps();
        UIALogger.logPass("Test passed");
    } catch(exception) {
        UIALogger.logError(exception.message);
        UIATarget.localTarget().logElementTree();
        UIALogger.logFail("Test failed");
        throw exception;
    }
}
```

To close the log group as a failure, we just throw an exception. If we don't and the function containing our steps executes without issues, the log group will be marked as successful.

Notice that we pass the function containing our test steps *inline* as the second argument. We could have given this function a name by assigning it to a variable and used that name as an argument to the test() function. But this inline function syntax is a common way to express behavior that you are delegating or deferring, similar to the way blocks are specified inline in Objective-C.

These first two tools are a great way to introduce our toolbox—we have a terse function to log neutral messages to the trace log, and we have a very simple way to declare and manage log groups. Let's continue and build a cleaner way to make assertions.

Quick and Simple Assertion Functions

While the capability to throw any exception we want as a failure message is powerful and simple, we can do better by making assertions a first-class concept in our test environment. Consider the following:

04-OrganizingTestCode/step05/automation/env.js
```
test("Build a better assertion", function() {
    var term = "fish";
    if (term != "coffee") {
        throw new Error("Expected coffee, but is '" + term + "'");
    }
});
```

We throw an error if term is not equal to "coffee". The intent is clear, but assertions like this will be so common that we should pull this kind of check into a top-level function:

04-OrganizingTestCode/step06/automation/env.js
```
function assert(value, failMsg) {
    if (value) return;
    if (!failMsg) failMsg = "Assert failed";
    throw new Error(failMsg);
}
```

Here we start with a guard clause to exit the assertion immediately if value is true. No need to raise a fuss in that case. If the value isn't true, then we check if we have a custom fail message, or use a default if one isn't supplied. Finally, we throw the message in an Error object like we've done before.

Now we can express our test like so:

```
04-OrganizingTestCode/step06/automation/env.js
test("Build a better assertion", function() {
    var term = "fish";
    assert(term == "coffee", "Expected coffee, but is '" + term + "'");
});
```

Since our conditional expression evaluates to false, assert() raises our failure message and we get the following error output and our log group fails, ending the test:

```
Expected coffee, but is 'fish'
```

We can use assert() for all our general-purpose needs, but testing for equality is such a common case that we can give it special treatment with customized output:

```
04-OrganizingTestCode/step07/automation/env.js
function assertEqual(value1, value2, failMsg) {
    if (value1 === value2) return;
    if (!failMsg) failMsg = "Assert Equal failed";
    var fullMsg = failMsg + ": '" + value1 + "'" +
        " !== '" + value2 + "'";
    assert(false, fullMsg);
}
```

This first line checks to see if the values are equal, and exits early if so. No sense in trying to build the failure message if there's no need. Notice that we're using ===. The double equal operator tries to coerce the values when checking for equality, so the string "0" would be equal to the integer zero, which also happens to be equal to the value false. That's often a confusing gotcha in JavaScript, so we're using the triple equal operator, which checks for equality without coercion for consistent results.

Because we're handling a specific kind of assertion, we can generate a more meaningful failure message to give us better context. We append the string representations of the two values passed in to the failure message, wrapping those values in single quotes for convenience. Say we invoke it this way:

```
04-OrganizingTestCode/step07/automation/env.js
test("Build a better assertion", function() {
    var term = "fish";
    assertEqual(term, "coffee", "Terms not equal");
});
```

We only have to reference term and "coffee" once in the line. The short failure message is all we need when the rest of the context is appended. Here's what we get when we run it:

```
Terms not equal: 'fish' !== 'coffee'
```

And, of course, we should handle the opposite case:

04-OrganizingTestCode/step07/automation/env.js
```
function assertNotEqual(value1, value2, failMsg) {
    if (value1 !== value2) return;
    if (!failMsg) failMsg = "Assert Not Equal failed";
    var fullMsg = failMsg + ": '" + value1 + "'" +
        " === '" + value2 + "'";
    assert(false, fullMsg);
}
```

04-OrganizingTestCode/step07/automation/env.js
```
test("Build assertNotEqual", function() {
    var term = "fish";
    assertNotEqual(term, "fish", "Terms are the same");
});
```

Using these global assertion functions, we're developing a language, of sorts, to express our intent with as little friction as possible. Of course, we don't have to stop with just these tools. You'll most certainly have specific needs for your own projects.

Next, we'll discuss how to take something as complex as a whole application and break it up into conceptual pieces that help us describe what we want our tests to cover.

4.2 Describing the App with Screen Objects

Let's think through what we have so far. UI Automation provides a scripting interface to the application through a set of objects representing the window, controls, and device. We act on these objects with events, check the results on the screen, and log errors if they aren't what we expect.

Our test steps can become very verbose. The test's meaning gets clouded by complicated lookups and assertions. We need a way to hide the unnecessary stuff.

Because we are dealing with mobile user interfaces, we can break our problem up into "screens" that represent the different cognitive states of the user. In our vernacular, a screen may encompass the whole physical screen, or it could represent a modal view or a list in a sidebar. Regardless, if we build our tests by interacting with these screens, we will have a language built into our test code that is easier to read and write, and a natural way to encapsulate the test behavior and assertions.

Let's experiment with screen objects by converting each of our three existing tests to use them. Just like UI Automation exposes elements as representations of controls on the screen, we'll create objects as representations of our screens and all the things they know and do.

Since our tests are going to be so brief, we'll put all of them in the same file instead of breaking them into separate files. Create a script file named automation/test_suite.js where we will rewrite our test suite as we convert it. Let's start by rethinking the test to add a search term to the list:

```
04-OrganizingTestCode/step08/automation/test_suite.js
#import "env.js";
test("Putting the 'coffee' term back in the list", function() {
    SearchTermScreen.addTerm('coffee');
    SearchTermScreen.assertTerm(0, 'coffee');
});
```

We're using our test-grouping function that we wrote in the last section, but rather than just paste in all the code for the test that we wrote before, we're experimenting with how we could express the intent of the test in just a couple of meaningful lines.

The SearchTermScreen.addTerm() method is a higher-level step that bundles up all of the lower-level steps to do the work. Once we define this we can use it anywhere, even in performance tests. If the lower-level steps to add a term change (like if we move the button to the other side of the navigation bar), then we only have to update the one place that knows what addTerm() means.

Likewise, the concept of asserting a specific term involves looking up a table view cell and checking to see if it is valid. By pulling those details into the SearchTermScreen.assertTerm() method, we're left with a higher-level step in our test saying that the top search term must be "coffee."

We could just as easily build global functions like log() and assert() to do this dirty work, but then it's possible that we could end up with naming clashes. By putting them on a screen object we are giving them a namespace. For simple tests like this we don't even have to write out the full name of the object. We can assign it to a short variable name, like so:

```
04-OrganizingTestCode/step09/automation/test_suite.js
#import "env.js";
test("Putting the 'coffee' term back in the list", function() {
    var s = SearchTermScreen;
    s.addTerm('coffee');
    s.assertTerm(0, 'coffee');
});
```

We can get carried away with this, of course, and if we had many screens to interact with at once I'd advise caution when doing this. Still, the technique is there and gives us options for how to express our tests. The point of using screen objects is to namespace methods that help us describe the step we are doing at a higher level.

Building Our First Screen Object

So, how do these screen objects work? Let's start constructing the representation of our search-term list:

04-OrganizingTestCode/step09/automation/lib/screens/SearchTermScreen.js

```
var SearchTermScreen = {
    addTerm: function(name) {
        log("Showing alert to add search term");
        var target = UIATarget.localTarget();
        var app = target.frontMostApp();
        UIATarget.onAlert = function() {
            return true;
        };
        app.navigationBar().rightButton().tap();
        app.keyboard().typeString(name);
        app.alert().defaultButton().tap();
    },
    // ...
};
```

Objects in JavaScript are simply dictionaries with a little bit of extra behavior available to them. In this case we are filling the variable SearchTermScreen with a dictionary that has one key, addTerm, and an anonymous function as the value. In JavaScript these keys can be accessed like object properties, and if a property contains a function, that function will be bound to the object as a method.

I like to choose method names that help describe what users are thinking of doing when they act. Here we have the method addTerm(), where we paste in the relevant portion of the test we wrote in Section 3.1, *Testing with a Modal Alert View*, on page 23. Instead of hard-coding the search-term name like we did before, we accept it as an argument.

Now we're ready to write our assertion method. We want to assert that a term is at a certain index:

04-OrganizingTestCode/step09/automation/lib/screens/SearchTermScreen.js

```
var SearchTermScreen = {
    // ...
    assertTerm: function(index, term) {
        log("Checking for", term, "at index", index);
        var target = UIATarget.localTarget();
        var app = target.frontMostApp();
        var window = app.mainWindow();
        var cell = window.tableViews()[0].cells()[index];
        assertEqual(cell.name(), term);
    }
};
```

We're using our log() method to let us know what we're about to do. We grab the target, app, and window, and then grab the cell at the given index to assert if the name equals term. If the assertion fails, the error message we crafted earlier will be thrown, and caught by our test() function that wraps everything in a log group. Now we're really starting to see our toolbox work.

To access this screen object, we need to import it into our test-environment file:

04-OrganizingTestCode/step09/automation/env.js
```
// Import screen files into our test environment
#import "lib/screens/SearchTermScreen.js";
```

Since we are importing env.js at the top of our test suite, our entire test environment gets pulled in and set up for us to use. If we run automation/features/add_search_term.js in UI Automation, a new search term will be added and checked, just like before.

Yet we have a dilemma. We're *still* doing a lot of boilerplate fetching that we know *every* screen-object method will have to do. Before, our test was written in a linear fashion and the intermediate variables we used to hold the app and window elements were available everywhere. We could declare them globally, but how do we know if they are fresh? What is a clean and simple way to pull these out for reuse?

Let's expand our SearchTermScreen object with methods that fetch common UI elements for us every time:

04-OrganizingTestCode/step10/automation/lib/screens/SearchTermScreen.js
```
var SearchTermScreen = {

    addTerm: function(name) {
        log("Showing alert to add search term");
        UIATarget.onAlert = function() {
            return true;
        };
        this.navigationBar().rightButton().tap();
        this.app().keyboard().typeString(name);
        this.app().alert().defaultButton().tap();
    },
    assertTerm: function(index, name) {
        log("Checking for", name, "at index", index);
        var cell = this.window().tableViews()[0].cells()[index];
        assertEqual(cell.name(), name);
    },

    // Helper methods
```

```
    target: function() {
        return UIATarget.localTarget();
    },
    app: function() {
        return this.target().frontMostApp();
    },
    navigationBar: function() {
        return this.app().navigationBar();
    },
    window: function() {
        return this.app().mainWindow();
    }
};
```

Notice the this keyword. It is just like self in Objective-C. The functions we specify here are *bound* to this object, and that's what gives this its special meaning.

These are such common operations that extracting them like this will pay off. When we call the navigationBar() method, it calls the app() method, which calls the target() method that starts the lookup down the chain. As a result, we are guaranteed to have a fresh element representing what is on the screen, and we don't have to assign all those intermediate variables.

Now that we've established these common methods to retrieve what we want, we can leverage JavaScript's object model to help us reuse them. Let's explore how to make a generic screen object so we can reuse common methods.

4.3 Reusing a Generic Screen Prototype

Objects aren't instances manufactured out of class templates by the runtime like in Objective-C. In JavaScript, objects are built on the fly and share behavior based on *prototypes*. In this section, we're going to leverage this to simplify how we define our screen objects.

Let's pull out all the common methods we want into a generic Screen object:

04-OrganizingTestCode/step11/automation/lib/screens/Screen.js
```
var Screen = {

    target: function() {
        return UIATarget.localTarget();
    },
    app: function() {
        return this.target().frontMostApp();
    },
    window: function() {
        return this.app().mainWindow();
    },
```

```
    navigationBar: function() {
        return this.app().navigationBar();
    },
    toolbar: function() {
        return this.app().toolbar();
    }
};
```

Just like we did before, we're defining all these helper methods as properties on an object instance assigned to the variable Screen.

Here's where the magic happens. We can clean up our SearchTermScreen object and only leave behind the two methods that are unique to this screen's behavior. Then we *change its prototype* to be the generic Screen object we defined previously.

04-OrganizingTestCode/step11/automation/lib/screens/SearchTermScreen.js

```
var SearchTermScreen = {

    addTerm: function(name) {
        log("Showing alert to add search term");
        UIATarget.onAlert = function() {
            return true;
        };
        this.navigationBar().rightButton().tap();
        this.app().keyboard().typeString(name);
        this.app().alert().defaultButton().tap();
    },

    assertTerm: function(index, name) {
        log("Checking for", name, "at index", index);
        var cell = this.window().tableViews()[0].cells()[index];
        assertEqual(cell.name(), name);
    }
};
```

➤ SearchTermScreen.__proto__ = Screen;

Now SearchTermScreen contains the specific properties unique to it and *inherits* Screen's properties. If we need to ensure that a method is available on all screen objects, we just put a property for it on Screen, and it will show up on any object with that prototype.

There are many ways to construct objects in JavaScript. I'm introducing the simplest here since we only need single instances of these screen objects. We want to reuse properties, and altering prototypes of instances satisfies that need well.

How do you know what should go in this generic object versus the specific screens? My usual rubric leads me to choose the most common pieces. Every screen object will need access to the app and window. Every screen in this particular app has navigation bars and toolbars. For me, that is sufficient reason to put those methods here.

Because we're extracting Screen into a new file, we'll need to add that file to our list of imported files in env.js:

04-OrganizingTestCode/step11/automation/env.js
```
// Import screen files into our test environment
#import "lib/screens/Screen.js";
#import "lib/screens/SearchTermScreen.js";
```

Through all this, we've refactored our SearchTermScreen object and pulled out common pieces into a generic Screen prototype. Now we can reuse this to build the remaining screen objects we need for these tests.

4.4 Converting Our Test Suite to Screen Objects

Now that our toolbox is getting handier, we can quickly update the old test that removes a search term. Let's do some more experimentation and plan out the new test in the new test-suite file to replace the old one:

04-OrganizingTestCode/step12/automation/test_suite.js
```
test("Removing the 'coffee' search term", function() {
    var s = SearchTermScreen;
    s.removeTerm("coffee");
    s.assertNoTerm("coffee");
});
```

Pretty straightforward. We only have two high-level steps to perform. Neither the removeTerm() nor the assertNoTerm() method exists yet, so let's start by building removeTerm() on the SearchTermScreen object:

04-OrganizingTestCode/step12/automation/lib/screens/SearchTermScreen.js
```
// ...

removeTerm: function(name) {
    log("Removing search term", name);
    var editButton = this.navigationBar().leftButton();
    editButton.tap();

    var tableView = this.window().tableViews()[0];
    var cell = tableView.cells()[name];

    var deleteSwitch = cell.switches()[0];
    deleteSwitch.tap();
```

```
    var deleteButton = cell.buttons()[0];
    deleteButton.tap();

    editButton.tap();
},

// ...
```

Nothing unfamiliar here. We're just doing what we did before to find the search-term cell and delete it, but this time we're leveraging the Screen prototype helper methods and our log() function to do the dirty work.

Our assertion method is going to take different steps than we took manually in our original test. Before, we had a reference to the cell we deleted saved in a variable. We called waitForInvalid() on it to pause until it vanished from the screen, and then asked the element if it was indeed invalid. Because we're always fetching fresh elements from the target, we can simply try to fetch the cell by name again and check the result:

04-OrganizingTestCode/step12/automation/lib/screens/SearchTermScreen.js
```
// ...

assertNoTerm: function(name) {
    log("Assert no term named", name);
    this.target().pushTimeout(0.1);
    var tableView = this.window().tableViews()[0];
    var cell = tableView.cells()[name];
    this.target().popTimeout();
    assert(!cell.isValid(), "Cell still there");
},

// ...
```

We're pushing the short timeout so the query won't take very long, then we're looking up the cell by name again. Finally, we use our assert() function to check the cell's validity, and our work is done.

Converting the Search-Results Test

Like before, let's do a bit of work to reimagine the test that checked the list of results from the OpenStreetMap API:

04-OrganizingTestCode/step12/automation/test_suite.js
```
test("Searching for 'coffee' in downtown San Francisco", function() {
    SearchTermScreen.tapTerm("coffee");
    ResultsScreen.showList();
    ResultsListScreen.assertResult("Coffee Cabin, 0.6 mi");
    ResultsScreen.goBack();
});
```

We're getting a bit more complicated here because we're navigating between screens. We're tapping the specific search term, switching from the map to show the list on the results screen, asserting that a known result shows up in the list, and then telling our results screen that we want to go back.

Let's break this down one piece at a time. We're already familiar with the SearchTermScreen; we just need to add the new step to tap a search term:

04-OrganizingTestCode/step12/automation/lib/screens/SearchTermScreen.js
```
var SearchTermScreen = {

    // ...

    tapTerm: function(name) {
        var tableView = this.window().tableViews()[0];
        tableView.cells()[name].tap();
    }

};

SearchTermScreen.__proto__ = Screen;
```

We grab a copy of the table view in the window, look up the cell with the given name, and tap it, just as we did before. Because of the reusable pieces of our Screen prototype, our tapTerm() method is short and sweet.

Now we can start defining our ResultsScreen object. We'll do the same as before and make a new Screen object with a method for toggling the switch to show the list view:

04-OrganizingTestCode/step12/automation/lib/screens/ResultsScreen.js
```
"use strict";

var ResultsScreen = {
    showList: function() {
        log("Switching to the list of results");
        var toggle = this.toolbar().segmentedControls()[0];
        toggle.buttons()['List'].tap();
    }
};

ResultsScreen.__proto__ = Screen;
```

To trigger the list view, we look up the toolbar using the method inherited from the Screen prototype, find the first (and only) segmented control, and tap the button with the name List. The screen switches and we're ready to look through the list of results.

Now we reach a choice. We could represent the entire concept of results as a single screen object. There's not necessarily a right or wrong way to do this. But for the sake of argument, let's say we want to subdivide the results screen into its two components. Users are looking at either a map plotted with points of interest or a list of results. That's a good reason to justify two separate, additional screens in this case.

We're focusing on the list screen, so let's build it based on our Screen prototype:

```
04-OrganizingTestCode/step12/automation/lib/screens/ResultsListScreen.js
"use strict";

var ResultsListScreen = {
    assertResult: function(name) {
        log("Checking for list for result", name);
        var tableView = this.window().tableViews()[0];
        var cell = tableView.cells()[name];
        assert(cell.isValid(), "Result not found!");
    }
};


ResultsListScreen.__proto__ = Screen;
```

Just like we did before, we search for any cell that matches the given name, and assert that the result we get back is valid. Because we are using the fetching methods on our Screen prototype, we know we're guaranteed a fresh representation of the UI every time.

Now that we've navigated to the results list and made our assertion, we can unwind our test and go back to the search-term screen. Because the concept of tapping the Back button is part of the containing ResultsScreen, let's put a method on it that taps that button:

```
04-OrganizingTestCode/step12/automation/lib/screens/ResultsScreen.js
var ResultsScreen = {
    goBack: function() {
        var backButton = this.navigationBar().leftButton();
        backButton.tap();
    },

    // ...
};
```

It might seem pedantic to build a method that is this simple. We could just as easily access the navigation bar directly from our test() function and avoid this entirely. But I find that method names like this are as much descriptive of the intentions as they are wrappers of the behavior. We mean "go back out of this screen," so for our purposes here, that's what we're encoding in the name of this higher-level step.

And that's it. Run the new automation/test_suite.js to make sure everything works, and then throw away the old scripts. We've simplified our tests with a reusable toolbox built on top of what UI Automation and JavaScript give us. We'll be extending this as we go.

Choosing the Tools that Work

These techniques have served me well on projects I've contributed to that are available from the App Store. But don't take what you see here as dogma. The beauty of walking through this together is that we get to see how all the pieces can be assembled. If you need to write a test and building a screen object seems like more effort than it's worth for a certain step, then punt on it. Use the tools to write clear tests. Ignore the ones that don't help.

The UI Automation developer community is small, but growing. Lots of other JavaScript libraries and tools out there might be useful. But remember, this isn't one of the popular JavaScript runtime environments, like web browsers or Node. I think it's best to grasp what you're doing in JavaScript yourself, and *then* look toward other libraries to help clean up your ideas when you're ready. Grabbing a third-party library before you fully understand it is a kind of premature optimization. It could hurt more than it helps.

Tuneup JS, by Alex Vollmer, is a great library to continue exploring the themes we've covered in this chapter.[2] Alex also uses a test() method to group steps together, and does more complicated assertions. He even has a way to assert that a whole screen is laid out according to a JavaScript dictionary describing a view hierarchy. There is a lot to learn from, and it's a small enough testing library that I encourage JavaScript beginners to read through it. You'll pick up a lot of good concepts.

Build your toolbox slowly. Don't be afraid to try out ideas for a bit. When you see yourself using the same pattern a few times, then it might be worthwhile to consider how to extract it into something generic. Growing a test suite is just like growing production code. Small steps are better. Build often. Refactor and reorganize for clarity. These steps are for you, because you're the one who has to read and maintain these tests.

In the next chapter we'll expand on the tools we've built here and dig into using gestures, map views, and the accessibility APIs to our advantage.

---

2.   http://www.tuneupjs.org

CHAPTER 5

Maps, Gestures, and Alerts

NearbyMe makes heavy use of Apple's Map Kit framework to provide the map view that the user manipulates, and we should assume it works as described. However, we don't want to distract ourselves by testing the implementation of Map Kit; we want to test how *we* interact with it in our code.

We're going to write two more tests for our test suite, covering the most common uses. First, we want to make sure that tapping a search term will execute a geographical query and actually show pins representing points of interest on the map. Second, we want to test what users see if they move and refresh the map *but there are no results*. The pins should be removed and users should see an alert letting them know that there's nothing found here. These two tests will help cover our critical code paths for the average use cases.

We'll need to dig deeper into UI Automation's rules to understand how UIView objects are represented as UIAElement objects through the accessibility APIs. To move the map around, we'll experiment with relatively complicated gestures like pinching and flicking. We'll need to build an alert-handler mechanism that lets us assert that specific alerts pop up to notify the user. When we're done, we'll have two more tests in our growing test suite!

5.1 Exploring the Map

We've already tested the list table view of results in Chapter 4, *Organizing Test Code*, on page 41, so we know that we're talking to the OpenStreetMap API correctly. We now need to make sure we're plotting the pins visibly on the map. We haven't interacted with the map yet; let's start by exploring how UI Automation represents it to us.

Start up the application in Instruments with the UI Automation template and switch to the script editor. Set up a script named sandbox.js in the automation directory. We'll use this as a place to play with these ideas before we clean them up and promote them to the test_suite.js file where our official tests live. In sandbox.js, turn on strict mode and import our test environment so we have our tools available:

05-MapsGestures/step01/automation/sandbox.js
```
"use strict";
#import "env.js";
```

Now, let's fetch the local target and the main window so we have them on hand when we're ready to log the element tree:

05-MapsGestures/step01/automation/sandbox.js
```
var target = UIATarget.localTarget();
var window = target.frontMostApp().mainWindow();
```

We'll hide these in a map screen object eventually, but while we're exploring, it doesn't hurt to write everything out long-form. As we see patterns emerge, we can pull out the common pieces for reuse.

Next we need to navigate from the initial list of search terms to the map of results. Since we're bringing our test toolbox with us by importing the test environment we started in Chapter 4, *Organizing Test Code*, on page 41, we can use the SearchTermScreen object to do the work:

05-MapsGestures/step01/automation/sandbox.js
```
SearchTermScreen.tapTerm("coffee");
```

Now let's log the whole window's element tree so we see what shows up when the map becomes visible:

05-MapsGestures/step01/automation/sandbox.js
```
var target = UIATarget.localTarget();
var window = target.frontMostApp().mainWindow();
SearchTermScreen.tapTerm("coffee");
➤ window.logElementTree();
```

Make sure that Run on Record is checked in the UI Automation sidebar, use the ⌘-R shortcut to stop, and press it again to restart the Instruments trace so the script plays back from the top of the application launch. The search term is tapped and the map slides into place. However, when we inspect the element tree in the log output, we don't see any of our pins! We see a representation of the map view and a couple more unrelated elements, as in Figure 25, *Logged element tree before fetch was complete*, on page 61, but that's it.

We don't see elements for our pins because the network request hadn't finished talking to the API by the time we logged the element tree. We have to put in a pause to let the user interface catch up. Let's add a five-second delay:

```
UIAWindow: rect:{{0, 0}, {320, 480}}
    UIANavigationBar: name:coffee rect:{{0, 20}, {320, 44}}
    UIAElement: name:Current Location rect:{{-2, 234}, {23, 23}}
    UIAMapView: rect:{{0, 64}, {320, 372}}
    UIAStaticText: name:Legal value:Legal rect:{{11, 416}, {24, 11}}
    UIAToolbar: rect:{{0, 436}, {320, 44}}
```

Figure 25—Logged element tree before fetch was complete

05-MapsGestures/step02/automation/sandbox.js
```
var target = UIATarget.localTarget();
var window = target.frontMostApp().mainWindow();
SearchTermScreen.tapTerm("coffee");
target.delay(5);     // Adjust to give network time to fetch
window.logElementTree();
```

Now running the test shows elements that represent the search results in the element tree. However, as we see in Figure 26, *Finding the map pins in the window*, on page 61, they *are not inside* the map element!

```
UIAWindow: rect:{{0, 0}, {320, 480}}
    UIANavigationBar: name:coffee rect:{{0, 20}, {320, 44}}
    UIAElement: name:Peet's Coffee rect:{{302, 69}, {32, 39}}
    UIAElement: name:Peet's Coffee and Tea rect:{{216, 162}, {32, 39}}
    UIAElement: name:Starbucks Coffee rect:{{216, 173}, {32, 39}}
    UIAElement: name:The Coffee Bean & Tea Leaf rect:{{166, 211}, {32, 39}}
    UIAElement: name:Chatz Coffee rect:{{252, 204}, {32, 39}}
    UIAElement: name:Tully's Coffee rect:{{278, 225}, {32, 39}}
    UIAElement: name:Current Location rect:{{148, 238}, {23, 23}}
    UIAElement: name:Emile's Coffee & Tea rect:{{5, 261}, {32, 39}}
    UIAElement: name:HRD Coffee Shop rect:{{282, 286}, {32, 39}}
    UIAElement: name:Rancho Parnassus Coffee rect:{{137, 301}, {32, 39}}
    UIAElement: name:Starbucks Coffee rect:{{266, 322}, {32, 39}}
    UIAMapView: rect:{{0, 64}, {320, 372}}
    UIAStaticText: name:Legal value:Legal rect:{{11, 416}, {24, 11}}
    UIAToolbar: rect:{{0, 436}, {320, 44}}
```

Figure 26—Finding the map pins in the window

Although this may seem odd, it has to do with the way that the map view represents the subelements through the accessibility framework. UI Automation observes and talks to our app using the same mechanisms as assistive technologies like VoiceOver. In this case, Apple wanted to have all the pins returned as peers of the map view. In a moment we'll touch on how we can use these accessibility APIs to our advantage.

Now that we know how the map is represented, let's complete our experimental test by hand-rolling an assertion to check that a specific pin is there:

05-MapsGestures/step02/automation/sandbox.js
```
log("Asserting that a pin exists");
var name = "The Coffee Bean & Tea Leaf";
var pin = window.elements()[name];
assert(pin.isValid(), "Not found");
```

We're asking for all the window's child elements and querying for the first one with the expected name. Since we're testing against a live API, you'll want to substitute a name that passes the test for you. If pin.isValid() returns true, then this is a real element that satisfies the query we made. If it returns false, that means we received a UIAElementNil object back because there was no child element in the window with the given name. You can watch the test fail by changing the expected name to something that you know won't be on the map.

We have enough information now to simplify this test with a screen object representing our map of results.

Building a Map Screen Object

Remember from Section 4.4, *Converting Our Test Suite to Screen Objects*, on page 54, we started with two screen objects to represent the results we show to the user. We used a screen object for the entire view that toggles between the map and list, and a separate screen object to represent just the list with the table view of results. To continue that pattern, let's make a screen object to represent the map:

05-MapsGestures/step02/automation/lib/screens/ResultsMapScreen.js
```
"use strict";
var ResultsMapScreen = {
    assertPinNamed: function(name) {
        log("Looking up", name, "on the map");
        var elements = this.window().elements();
        var pin = elements[name];
        assert(pin.isValid(), "Not found");
    }
};
ResultsMapScreen.__proto__ = Screen;
```

We're building our ResultsMapScreen object and setting its prototype to our base Screen object that has the helper methods for element lookup. By starting the assertPinName() method with a log message, we keep track of what we're trying to assert as we read through the trace log. We look up the window using this.window() provided by our Screen prototype, try to find the pin by name, and assert if the returned element is valid or not.

We need to import this new screen into our env.js test-environment file so it's available everywhere we need it:

05-MapsGestures/step02/automation/env.js
```
// Import screen files into our test environment
#import "lib/screens/Screen.js";
#import "lib/screens/SearchTermScreen.js";
#import "lib/screens/ResultsScreen.js";
#import "lib/screens/ResultsListScreen.js";
#import "lib/screens/ResultsMapScreen.js";
```

Now we can write a new test at the end of test_suite.js, asserting that a specific pin shows up in the results map screen:

05-MapsGestures/step02/automation/test_suite.js
```
test("Searching for 'coffee' on the map in San Francisco", function() {
    SearchTermScreen.tapTerm("coffee");
    ResultsMapScreen.assertPinNamed("The Coffee Bean & Tea Leaf");
    ResultsScreen.goBack();
});
```

We're interacting with the search-term screen like before to tap the term we want, and then we're using the results map screen we just wrote to assert that a pin we expect shows up on the map. As before, you'll want to substitute a pin name that passes the test for you since we're talking to a live API that could change by the time you read this. We finish the test by navigating back out of the results so that the next test is ready to run from a common starting point.

Notice that we don't need the delay anymore like we did in our earlier experiment. By querying for a pin with a specific name, we're leaning on the default system timeout. Whenever you can, use this timeout mechanism to your advantage. You don't need to reinvent your own screen-polling solution for scenarios the system can handle for you.

Run the test-suite script by pressing ⌘-R twice to restart the application in Instruments. We're greeted with four passing tests. Now that we've seen a bit about how the map and pins work, let's cover how to change the representation of those pins through the accessibility APIs in Objective-C.

5.2   Identifying Elements with Accessibility APIs

Our test works fine for the moment, but we have a fragile situation on our hands. As we see in Figure 26, *Finding the map pins in the window*, on page 61, the pin annotation views are represented as just plain UIAElement instances. Although we're able to use the special filtering methods such as buttons() and cells() to fetch only elements of a certain type, we don't have that convenience here. We have to use the generic elements() method.

This could be a problem if we were testing for a pin with the name Legal, for instance, because the static text element for the Map Kit legal disclaimer has that name and is a sibling in the element array, along with all our pins. This could give us a false positive in a test. We need a better way to uniquely identify our pins.

To address this, we're going to experiment with the accessibility APIs to understand how UI Automation sees UIAElement instances. We'll be jumping back and forth between Objective-C and JavaScript a bit, but it will pay off because we'll have a much more reliable way to distinguish our pins from the other elements on the screen.

The accessibility APIs are the basis for technologies like VoiceOver that give visually impaired users a better experience. You can specify traits to identify elements as buttons, search fields, adjustable controls, or anything else that a user would need to manipulate on the screen.

We will use the accessibility APIs to define identifiers for our test's use that are separate from what the user can see and hear. By conforming to the UIAccessibilityIdentification *informal protocol*, any UIView subclass can change the value of the name() method on its UIAElement representation. This protocol is informal because we don't have to declare it in the Objective-C class interface. We merely have to define a method with the name accessibilityIdentifier in a subclass.

Since Map Kit gives us full control over the annotation views that appear over the map, we can use a custom subclass of MKPinAnnotationView. Let's switch back to Xcode and change our map results view controller so it returns our subclass:

```
05-MapsGestures/step03/NearbyMe/NBMMapResultsViewController.m
- (MKAnnotationView *)mapView:(MKMapView *)mapView
          viewForAnnotation:(id<MKAnnotation>)annotation
{
    if ([annotation isKindOfClass:[MKUserLocation class]]) {
      return nil;
```

```
    } else {
        MKPinAnnotationView *view = [[NBMAccessibleAnnotationView alloc]
                                     initWithAnnotation:annotation
                                     reuseIdentifier:nil];

        view.canShowCallout = YES;
        view.animatesDrop = YES;
        return view;
    }
}
```

As the delegate of the map view, this view controller will be asked for an annotation view for every annotation on the map. We first check to see if the given annotation represents the user's current location. If it does, we're just returning nil so the Map Kit framework can handle it the way it normally does, with the blue pulsating dot. If this isn't a user-location annotation, then we create an instance of our custom subclass, NBMAccessibleAnnotationView, and return it instead.

In our custom annotation view we return a new string for the accessibilityIdentifier:

05-MapsGestures/step03/NearbyMe/NBMAccessibleAnnotationView.m

```
@implementation NBMAccessibleAnnotationView

- (NSString *)accessibilityIdentifier
{
    NBMPointOfInterest *poi = self.annotation;
    return [NSString stringWithFormat:@"POI: %@", poi.title];
}

@end
```

We use the annotation that belongs to this annotation view and return a string of the annotation title prefixed with POI:. Remember that the accessibility identifier is not visible or audible to the user. We can put whatever we want in here to distinguish our elements.

We need to rebuild our application and load it in Instruments so our automation scripts can see this change. Choose Profile from the Product menu in Xcode or press ⌘-I, and the app will build and open in the Instruments trace document.

In the UI Automation script editor, let's write a quick script in our sandbox file that takes us to the map screen and logs the element tree so we can see what changed:

05-MapsGestures/step03/automation/sandbox.js

```
#import "env.js";

var target = UIATarget.localTarget();
var window = target.frontMostApp().mainWindow();
SearchTermScreen.tapTerm("coffee");
target.delay(5);     // Adjust to give network time to fetch
window.logElementTree();
```

We're tapping the search term and pausing for a moment so the network request can complete before logging the element tree. When we run our automation script by pressing ⌘-R twice to stop and restart the trace, we'll see output similar to what the following figure shows. This prefix gives us a reasonable way to uniquely distinguish points of interest from other elements.

```
▼ UIAWindow: rect:{{0, 0}, {320, 480}}
  ▶ UIANavigationBar: name:coffee rect:{{0, 20}, {320, 44}}
    UIAElement: name:POI: Peet's Coffee rect:{{302, 69}, {32, 39}}
    UIAElement: name:POI: Peet's Coffee and Tea rect:{{216, 162}, {32, 39}}
    UIAElement: name:POI: Starbucks Coffee rect:{{216, 173}, {32, 39}}
    UIAElement: name:POI: The Coffee Bean & Tea Leaf rect:{{166, 211}, {32, 39}}
    UIAElement: name:POI: Chatz Coffee rect:{{252, 204}, {32, 39}}
    UIAElement: name:POI: Tully's Coffee rect:{{278, 225}, {32, 39}}
    UIAElement: name:Current Location rect:{{148, 238}, {23, 23}}
    UIAElement: name:POI: Emile's Coffee & Tea rect:{{5, 261}, {32, 39}}
    UIAElement: name:POI: HRD Coffee Shop rect:{{282, 286}, {32, 39}}
    UIAElement: name:POI: Rancho Parnassus Coffee rect:{{137, 301}, {32, 39}}
    UIAElement: name:POI: Starbucks Coffee rect:{{266, 322}, {32, 39}}
    UIAMapView: rect:{{0, 64}, {320, 372}}
    UIAStaticText: name:Legal value:Legal rect:{{11, 416}, {24, 11}}
  ▶ UIAToolbar: rect:{{0, 436}, {320, 44}}
```

Figure 27—Prefixing POI: to pin identifiers

We need to change how our ResultsMapScreen object works, because it doesn't know about the POI: prefix yet. Let's do this by building a method specifically for looking up pins by name on the map:

05-MapsGestures/step03/automation/lib/screens/ResultsMapScreen.js

```
pinNamed: function(name) {
    log("Looking up", name, "on the map");
    var elements = this.window().elements();
    return elements["POI: " + name];
}
```

We're using simple string concatenation to add the prefix to the name passed in to our assertion. Since the ResultsMapScreen object encapsulates all the logic for looking up a point of interest by name, we can change the prefix of pin identifiers again if we need to. As long as we've used our screen objects in all the tests we write, we only have to make the update for the new pin identifiers in this one file.

Now we can update our assertion to use the new method:

```
05-MapsGestures/step03/automation/lib/screens/ResultsMapScreen.js
assertPinNamed: function(name) {
    assert(this.pinNamed(name).isValid(), "Not found");
},
```

Run the whole test suite again to make sure nothing is broken; everything passes!

The accessibility APIs are a powerful ally when working with automation scripts. Changing the accessibilityIdentifier on view objects is a great way to help solve ambiguity. There are many more ways to use these APIs to your advantage, such as by defining containers of elements for nonview objects and hiding views from the element tree entirely. Adapting these representations to your application improves the user experience and makes it easier to access elements in your tests. Check Apple's documentation for more information.[1]

Now that we've studied the map and how elements are represented, we're ready to start writing our final acceptance test for this chapter and learning a bit about simulated gestures along the way.

5.3 Testing with Gestures

For this next test, we want to make sure that no pins show up on the screen when there are no results. There are a couple of ways to do this. We could create a gobbledygook search term that we're confident won't return anything. Instead let's make this test cover a little bit more behavior by moving the map over the ocean and refreshing the results. This helps us check to make sure our search queries use the map bounds and that refreshing removes existing pins.

The gestures described in the following figure make it happen. Pinch to zoom out, and then flick the map over to the right. Once we tap the refresh button in the toolbar, we'll check for the alert view that pops up and assert that no points of interest show up on the map.

---

1. http://developer.apple.com/library/ios/documentation/UserExperience/Conceptual/iPhoneAccessibility/Accessibility_on_iPhone/Accessibility_on_iPhone.html

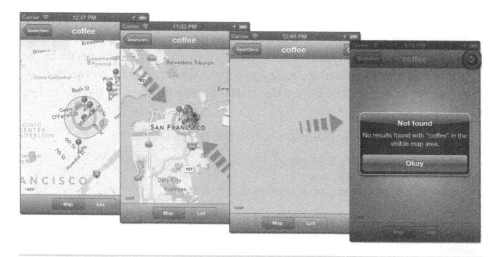

Figure 28—Refreshing over the ocean

Pinching and Zooming

Let's begin by clearing out the sandbox.js file so we have a blank slate for more experimentation. We'll try out a set of gestures before we pull the reusable pieces out into our map screen object. First, fetch all the usual variables and tap the "coffee" search term to navigate to the map:

```
05-MapsGestures/step04/automation/sandbox.js
"use strict";
#import "env.js";

var target = UIATarget.localTarget();
var window = target.frontMostApp().mainWindow();
SearchTermScreen.tapTerm("coffee");
target.delay(3);    // Adjust to give map time for first animation
```

We're pausing for three seconds after the transition to the map view because we don't want to start the pinch gesture right away. This particular app animates an initial map zoom to show users where they are. We don't want to interrupt that for this test.

Once the delay is done, we fetch the map view from the window:

```
05-MapsGestures/step04/automation/sandbox.js
var mapView = window.mapViews()[0];
```

We know from looking at the element tree earlier that the map is a direct subelement of the main window. We ask the window for just the map views and grab the first one, saving it into a variable.

We've triggered simple gestures before by calling the tap() method on individual elements. Pinch gesture events, on the other hand, can only be sent to the UIATarget itself. Gestures triggered on the target can happen anywhere and are specified in absolute screen coordinates. This comes in handy if you need to interact *outside* the application views, like tapping the raw screen coordinates over the status bar to force a scroll view to return its content offset to the top.

To pinch just the map, we need to get its coordinates on the screen and calculate where the touches will travel inside of it, like so:

05-MapsGestures/step04/automation/sandbox.js
```
var rect = mapView.rect();
var mapCenter = {
    x: rect.size.width/2 + rect.origin.x,
    y: rect.size.height/2 + rect.origin.y
};
var startPoint = {
    x: mapCenter.x - 60,
    y: mapCenter.y
};
var endPoint = {
    x: mapCenter.x,
    y: mapCenter.y
};
target.pinchCloseFromToForDuration(startPoint, endPoint, 3);
```

The pinchCloseFromToForDuration() method takes three parameters: two points to indicate how the pinch travels across the screen, and the duration of the gesture in seconds. For the sake of clarity, we're using the intermediate variables startPoint and endPoint and calculating them relative to the mapCenter variable so we can easily see what the gesture coordinates are composed of.

The first point acts like a movable finger that travels to meet the second point, an immovable finger on the screen. We start sixty points to the left of center and pinch toward the stationary point at the dead center of the map, like we see in Figure 29, *Pinching two points together*, on page 70.

Flicking Inside an Element

Now that we've zoomed out, we need to move away from land over to the empty ocean. Let's perform a flick gesture on the map element:

05-MapsGestures/step04/automation/sandbox.js
```
var options = {
    startOffset: {x:0.2, y:0.5},
    endOffset:   {x:0.9, y:0.4}
};
mapView.flickInsideWithOptions(options);
```

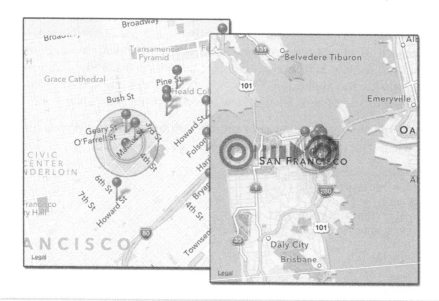

Figure 29—Pinching two points together

We call flickInsideWithOptions() on the UIAMapView object and provide a JavaScript dictionary with start and end offsets. Unlike the system-wide gestures performed on the UIATarget element, gestures performed on UIAElement objects use relative coordinates instead of screen coordinates.

These relative coordinates go from {x:0.0, y:0.0} in the top-left corner to {x:1.0, y:1.0} in the bottom right. Here we are saying that we want to initiate a flick, starting on the left side of the map and ending it over to the right while sloping up just a bit.

For a flick gesture like this, the distance between the points affects the momentum of the map as it moves. Flicking farther makes the map travel faster and farther before it rests. Here we're flicking across the width of the whole map to ensure that we end up far out to sea.

With our map in the right place, we need to press the refresh button by drilling down to find it in the navigation bar:

05-MapsGestures/step04/automation/sandbox.js
```
target.frontMostApp().navigationBar().rightButton().tap();
```

Running this script in the sandbox shows the map zoom out, move over the ocean, and refresh before letting us know that there's nothing to be found out there.

Using the Gestures in Screen Objects

Since we've proven out what the test steps should do, let's move them into our screen objects to clean things up. Let's replace the experiments we made in our sandbox.js file with a bit of experimentation for how we want the test to look:

```
05-MapsGestures/step05/automation/sandbox.js
#import "env.js";

test("Refreshing over the ocean returns no results", function() {
    SearchTermScreen.tapTerm("coffee");
    delay(3);    // Wait for the map to animate
    ResultsMapScreen.moveMapFarToTheLeft();
    ResultsScreen.tapRefreshButton();
});
```

We tap the search term, pause for the map to finish animating, move it to the far left over the ocean, and trigger the refresh. Only the first step of the test is already written, so let's start building the rest.

Now is a good time to create a delay() function to live alongside log(), test(), and the other global functions in our test-environment toolbox from Chapter 4, *Organizing Test Code*, on page 41. We won't need to use it often, but for some situations, like the initial zoom animation, we need to be explicit with the automation engine:

```
05-MapsGestures/step05/automation/env.js
function delay(seconds) {
    UIATarget.localTarget().delay(seconds);
}
```

Now let's bundle up the code for map interaction into methods on our ResultsMapScreen:

```
05-MapsGestures/step05/automation/lib/screens/ResultsMapScreen.js
var ResultsMapScreen = {
    // ...

    mapView: function() {
        return this.window().mapViews()[0];
    },

    moveMapFarToTheLeft: function() {
        var rect = this.mapView().rect();
        var mapCenter = {
            x: rect.size.width/2 + rect.origin.x,
            y: rect.size.height/2 + rect.origin.y
        };
```

```
        var startPoint = {
            x: mapCenter.x - 60,
            y: mapCenter.y
        };
        var endPoint = {
            x: mapCenter.x,
            y: mapCenter.y
        };
        this.target().pinchCloseFromToForDuration(startPoint, endPoint, 3);

        var options = {
            startOffset: {x:0.2, y:0.5},
            endOffset:   {x:0.9, y:0.4}
        };
        this.mapView().flickInsideWithOptions(options);
    }

};
```

We're starting with a method, mapView(), that we can use as the single source of truth to find the map view on the screen. We then write a method named after what the gestures are trying to do, moveMapFarToTheLeft(). If we needed to, we could break this down into more granular gesture steps, but we don't want to get ahead of ourselves. This is sufficient for our purposes.

Next we move the code to push the refresh button into the ResultsScreen object, which is responsible for the buttons in the navigation bar:

05-MapsGestures/step05/automation/lib/screens/ResultsScreen.js
```
var ResultsScreen = {
    // ...

    tapRefreshButton: function() {
        this.navigationBar().rightButton().tap();
    }

};
```

We've moved the map and triggered a refresh, but we're not yet asserting anything. Let's see how to check for the alert.

5.4 Advanced Alert-Handling

When we refresh the map over the ocean, an alert pops up letting the user know that nothing was found. To test for this behavior, we're going to dig deeper into handling alerts. We'll look into the differences between asynchronous and synchronous alert-handling and choose the technique that works best for us in these cases.

Asynchronous Handlers

We first worked with alerts in Section 3.1, *Testing with a Modal Alert View*, on page 23, where we set up a simple handler to return true so the system knew we wanted the alert to remain on the screen while we interacted with it. That gave us the power to *synchronously* interact with alerts. This time let's try asynchronous handling to see if it offers us a clearer way to express the test.

In our sandbox.js file, start by adding an alert handler *before* we tap the refresh button that checks for the title "Not found":

05-MapsGestures/step06/automation/sandbox.js
```
test("Refreshing over the ocean returns no results", function() {
    SearchTermScreen.tapTerm("coffee");
    delay(3);    // Wait for the map to animate
    ResultsMapScreen.moveMapFarToTheLeft();

    UIATarget.onAlert = function(alert) {
        log("Checking for alert with title \"Not found\"");
        assertEqual("Not found", alert.staticTexts()[0].value());
        return false;
    };

    ResultsScreen.tapRefreshButton();
});
```

We're creating an alert handler that starts with a quick message and then asserts on the alert title. In some cases, you may want to assert on more details than that, but this is sufficient for us. We're returning false from this handler because it's fine to have the system dismiss the alert for us. We could have just as easily tapped the button to dismiss it ourselves.

When we run this, we see the map zoom out and move over the ocean, but when we inspect the log we see something like the following figure.

Log Messages	Log Type
▼ Refreshing over the ocean returns no results	Pass
target.frontMostApp().mainWindow().tableViews()[0].cells()["coffee"].tap()	Debug
target.pinchCloseFromToForDuration({x:"100", y:"250"}, {x:"160", y:"250"}, "3")	Debug
target.frontMostApp().mainWindow().mapViews()[0].flickInsideWithOptions({startOffs...	Debug
target.frontMostApp().mainWindow().mapViews()[0].scrollToVisible()	Debug
target.frontMostApp().navigationBar().rightButton().tap()	Debug
Test passed	Pass

Figure 30—The alert handler didn't have time to run.

The log message we tried to print at the start of the handler isn't there. Our alert handler was never called, yet the test passed! This is because we're using asynchronous alert-handling and our script ended *before the alert actually showed up on the screen*. The scripting runtime thought it was finished and cleaned up. When the alert finally did show up, our script was already done and nothing was executed.

To continue handling the alert asynchronously, we need to add a delay after we tap the refresh button. While we're at it, let's use a local variable as a semaphore to check if the alert handler was called:

05-MapsGestures/step07/automation/sandbox.js

```
var alertShown = false;
UIATarget.onAlert = function(alert) {
    log("Checking for alert with title \"Not found\"");
    assertEqual("Not found", alert.staticTexts()[0].value());
    alertShown = true;
    return false;
};

ResultsScreen.tapRefreshButton();
delay(3);
assert(alertShown, "Alert did not show");
```

The variable alertShown is accessible inside the alert handler's scope. Since we're adding a three-second delay after we tap the refresh button, the scripting engine should pause long enough for an alert to pop up. By the time the script resumes after the delay, the alert handler should have set the variable to true if it had been called. By writing an assertion on the value of alertShown, we protect ourselves from the test silently passing like it did before. We have two assertions: one for the alert title and one for the alert pop-up.

Synchronous Handlers

Asynchronous alert-handling is useful when we want to handle something that *might* happen, such as an alert that you want to get out of the way to keep the test steps moving. In this case, we *do* care whether the alert shows up. Let's look at how we would handle this synchronously and how it simplifies the test flow:

05-MapsGestures/step08/automation/sandbox.js

```
test("Refreshing over the ocean returns no results", function() {
    SearchTermScreen.tapTerm("coffee");
    delay(3);    // Wait for the map to animate
    ResultsMapScreen.moveMapFarToTheLeft();
    UIATarget.onAlert = function() { return true; };
    ResultsScreen.tapRefreshButton();
```

```
➤        log("Checking for alert with title \"Not found\"");
➤        var app = UIATarget.localTarget().frontMostApp();
➤        var alert = app.alert();
➤        assert(alert.isValid(), "Alert didn't show");
➤        assertEqual("Not found", alert.staticTexts()[0].value());
➤        alert.defaultButton().tap();
     });
```

We first set an alert handler that simply returns true, telling the system to leave the alert alone; then we tap the refresh button. This time, instead of delaying and doing our assertions in the alert handler, we ask the scripting interface to find the alert for us. By calling app.alert(), we ensure that the system will try to grab whatever alert is visible on the screen. If it's not there yet, it will keep polling up to the default timeout. We don't need a manual delay anymore.

When we get an object back from app.alert(), we can check to see if it is valid. If no alert was visible onscreen, we get back a UIAElementNil, and isValid() will return false. Assuming we have a valid UIAAlert object, we assert the value of the first static text we find. If the assertion passes, we tap the default button to dismiss the alert.

This synchronous handler is better for this test because the steps and expectations flow from top to bottom. There's less potential for confusion than with the asynchronous way, so we'll stick with this.

Extracting to an AlertScreen Object

Asserting that a specific alert showed up on the screen is such a common pattern that we'd do well to extract it into our test toolbox. Now that we've proven out how synchronous handling can work, let's start building an AlertScreen object that uses it:

05-MapsGestures/step09/automation/lib/screens/AlertScreen.js
```
"use strict";
var AlertScreen = {
    alert: function() {
        return this.app().alert();
    },
    assertWithTitle: function(expectedTitle) {
        log("Checking for an alert with title", expectedTitle);
        assert(this.alert().isValid(), "Alert didn't show");
        var title = this.alert().staticTexts()[0].value();
        assertEqual(title, expectedTitle);
    },
};
AlertScreen.__proto__ = Screen;
```

Like we started doing in Section 4.2, *Describing the App with Screen Objects*, on page 48, we're defining an object to represent what is on the screen and basing it on the reusable Screen prototype. Then we can build an assertWithTitle() method to find the alert, check that it is valid, and then check the title.

While we're here, let's also define the two actions we perform on alerts, confirming and canceling them:

05-MapsGestures/step09/automation/lib/screens/AlertScreen.js
```
var AlertScreen = {
    // ..

    confirm: function() {
        this.alert().defaultButton().tap();
    },

    cancel: function() {
        this.alert().cancelButton().tap();
    }
};
```

Before we can use it in our sandbox, we need to import this screen-object file in our env.js test-environment file:

05-MapsGestures/step09/automation/env.js
```
// Import screen files into our test environment
#import "lib/screens/Screen.js";
#import "lib/screens/SearchTermScreen.js";
#import "lib/screens/ResultsScreen.js";
#import "lib/screens/ResultsListScreen.js";
#import "lib/screens/ResultsMapScreen.js";
#import "lib/screens/AlertScreen.js";
```

And while we're editing our environment, let's assign the synchronous alert handler at the very top of the file:

05-MapsGestures/step09/automation/env.js
```
// We want to handle all alerts *synchronously* so return true to tell the
// system that we'll take care of it
UIATarget.onAlert = function() { return true; };
```

In this book, we don't have any need for the power of asynchronous alert-handling. By choosing the simpler synchronous version and wrapping the details of our interaction inside AlertScreen, we haven't given anything up that we need, and we can express the tests for alerts like so:

05-MapsGestures/step09/automation/sandbox.js
```
test("Refreshing over the ocean returns no results", function() {
    SearchTermScreen.tapTerm("coffee");
    delay(3);    // Wait for the map to animate
```

```
    ResultsMapScreen.moveMapFarToTheLeft();

    ResultsScreen.tapRefreshButton();

➤   AlertScreen.assertWithTitle("Not found");
➤   AlertScreen.confirm();
});
```

Much better. It's simple to read, and the logic for common interactions with alerts will be kept safe in one place. We're almost done with this test. The last thing we need to do is assert that there are no pins on the map.

No Pins? No Problem!

When we move the map out over the ocean and tap the refresh button, any pins that were there should be removed. Since we've already built our ResultsMapScreen, we can add an assertion for this as follows:

```
05-MapsGestures/step10/automation/lib/screens/ResultsMapScreen.js
var ResultsMapScreen = {
    // ...

    assertNoPins: function() {
        var predicate = "name beginswith \"POI: \"";
        this.target().pushTimeout(0.1);
        var pins = this.window().elements().withPredicate(predicate);
        assert(pins.length === 0, "Expected no pins on the map");
        this.target().popTimeout();
    },

    // ...
};
```

Remember back in Section 5.2, *Identifying Elements with Accessibility APIs*, on page 64 that we prefixed the identifiers of all our pins with POI:. We can exploit this for our purposes here by using the withPredicate() method on UIAElementArray to fetch and return a new array filtered to contain only elements that match the predicate expression. We're glossing over it a bit now, but we'll go deeper into how predicate expressions unlock new potential for us in Section 6.4, *Searching the Element Tree with Predicates*, on page 91.

Note that we're pushing a very short timeout. Unlike with our query for a specific pin, we *don't* want the system to keep polling the screen up to the default timeout. We expect the pins to vanish immediately, and we don't need the pause. We query for all the pins matching the predicate, assert that the length of the filtered UIAElementArray is zero, and then pop the timeout back to its original value.

Let's move our test out of the sandbox file to its final resting place in test_suite.js and add this last assertion to the end:

05-MapsGestures/step10/automation/test_suite.js

```
test("Refreshing over the ocean returns no results", function() {
    SearchTermScreen.tapTerm("coffee");
    delay(3);    // Wait for the map to animate
    ResultsMapScreen.moveMapFarToTheLeft();

    ResultsScreen.tapRefreshButton();

    AlertScreen.assertWithTitle("Not found");
    AlertScreen.confirm();

    ResultsMapScreen.assertNoPins();

    ResultsScreen.goBack();
});
```

As we've done before, we're tapping the Back button to return to the search-term screen so it plays well with future tests in this suite file. Run them all, watch them pass, and enjoy!

We've learned quite a few useful tricks. The accessibility APIs give us a lot of power to change how UIView subclasses are represented as elements. We experimented with more-complex gestures in relative and raw screen coordinates. We have a nice and simple way to assert that alerts match expectations, and we know for a fact that the test will fail if the alerts don't show up. Our map functionality has two useful acceptance tests covering the critical behavior the user needs.

Next we'll start testing our app running universally on the iPhone and iPad simulators and see how our test code needs to adapt for each device idiom.

CHAPTER 6

Strategies for Testing Universal Apps

NearbyMe is a hit with the customers. There's enough demand for an iPad version that we've decided to make it universal and run on both iPhone and iPad. Choosing to build a universal application presents a unique challenge —we now have to support two different user-interface idioms in one codebase.

Similarly, we have tough choices to make in our test code. Some of the scripts we've written are common enough to use for both device types without any modification. Inevitably, some will have to be changed to adapt. How do we know what to change? That depends on how much the two interface idioms share in common for any given application.

To answer that question, we'll examine the specific changes that make NearbyMe work on the iPad. The element tree will be different, so we'll need to explore it to understand what's happening. We'll port a couple of tests over to a new test suite built just for the iPad, reusing some parts of our test toolbox and adapting others. And we'll build a new tool to recursively find any element on the screen using the power of predicate expressions. By the time we're done, you'll have concrete steps you can take to grow universal test suites for your own applications.

6.1 Universalizing an Application

Apple's interface guidelines recommend against simply scaling up an iPhone app to fill the iPad screen. The extra screen space gives more room for complex gestures and to show previously hidden information. Different orientations give us new dimensions for presentation to the user. While common patterns are emerging in universal iOS apps today, every app has its own unique needs and constraints.

Let's look at how NearbyMe becomes universalized. The iPhone version uses a navigation view controller to let you "drill down" from the search-term list to the results. The results view controller itself is a container with two representations toggled by a switch: the map and the list of results. When you want to select a new search, you tap the Back button to "pop" back to the list of search terms. We can see this flow in the following figure.

Figure 31—iPhone app-navigation flow

On the iPad, however, we use the standard split view controller for navigation, as we see in the next figure. In landscape orientation, the *master view controller* is the search-term list on the left side. It is always visible, and tapping on a cell tells the *detail view controller* on the right-hand side to show the map of locations. Just like on the iPhone, the detail view controller is a container to toggle the results between the map and list representations.

Figure 32—iPad landscape app-navigation flow

Matters get more complicated in portrait orientation, as we see in the following figure. The split view controller *hides the master view controller* until shown by the user, who taps the button in the navigation bar or swipes from the left. Our users could get confused if they launch the app and see a blank screen, so we've decided to automatically show this master view controller in portrait orientation before users make their first selection. The net effect is that there is always a list of search terms on the screen at application launch time.

Figure 33—iPad portrait app-navigation flow

These "screens" of information are reused from the iPhone counterpart. We've made a pretty straightforward port from a navigation controller paradigm to a split view controller paradigm. Some apps undergo more radical changes to display and navigate information on the larger screen. We can't account for all the possibilities that you'll face in testing your own applications, but we can systematically walk through how to discover what we need to know to write new tests. Let's do that next.

6.2 Finding Elements in the New Idiom

Now that we've seen how NearbyMe changed to take advantage of the larger iPad screen, how has the element tree changed? Whenever we're faced with new interface designs to test, it's good to do some exploration and then pull the results out into our toolbox as we see fit. Let's try finding the list of search terms on the iPad and tapping one.

Make sure that Xcode is building for the iPad simulator and press ⌘-I to build and launch the app in Instruments. If the simulator was already running, make sure it is in portrait orientation.

Enter this script into the UI Automation instrument to try and tap the search term "coffee":

06-Universal/step01/automation/sandbox.js
```
"use strict";

var target = UIATarget.localTarget();
var window = target.frontMostApp().mainWindow();
var tableView = window.tableViews()[0];
var cell = tableView.cells()["coffee"];
cell.tap();
```

Make sure the Run on Record check box is turned on in the automation-instrument sidebar and press ⌘-R twice to stop and then start a new Instruments trace. After a moment we see a script error that looks like the following figure. When the script tried to ask for the table view cell with the name "coffee," it failed because we were calling the cells() method on a UIAElementNil object. Our request for the table view came up empty!

```
1   "use strict";
2
3   var target = UIATarget.localTarget();
4   var window = target.frontMostApp().mainWindow();
5   var tableView = window.tableViews()[0];
6   var cell = tableView.cells()["coffee"];
7   cell.tap();    Cannot perform action on invalid element: UIAElementNil from target.frontMostApp().mainWindow().tableViews()[0].cells()["coffee"]
8   |
```

Figure 34—Cannot find the table view in portrait orientation

To explore what changed, let's modify the script to log the whole window's element tree:

06-Universal/step02/automation/sandbox.js
```
"use strict";

var target = UIATarget.localTarget();
var window = target.frontMostApp().mainWindow();
```

➤ `window.logElementTree();`

Press ⌘-R to stop the trace and kill the application, and press it again to begin a new trace and run the script. We see a curious result in Figure 35, *Finding the popover element*, on page 83.

Our table view isn't a child of the window anymore. It is now a grandchild; a child of a UIAPopover element. Let's rewrite our little script to take this into account:

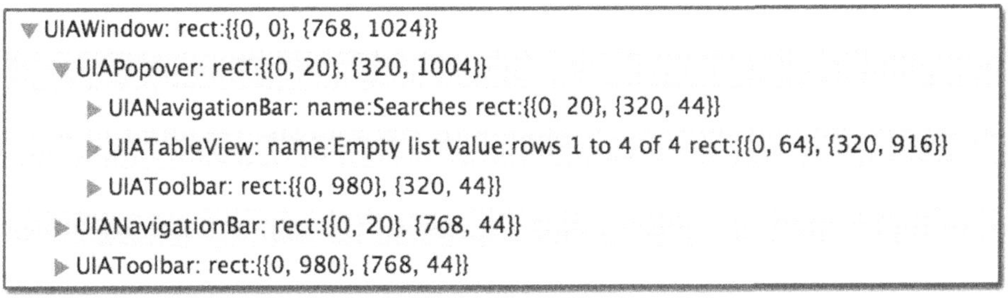

```
▼ UIAWindow: rect:{{0, 0}, {768, 1024}}
   ▼ UIAPopover: rect:{{0, 20}, {320, 1004}}
      ▶ UIANavigationBar: name:Searches rect:{{0, 20}, {320, 44}}
      ▶ UIATableView: name:Empty list value:rows 1 to 4 of 4 rect:{{0, 64}, {320, 916}}
      ▶ UIAToolbar: rect:{{0, 980}, {320, 44}}
   ▶ UIANavigationBar: rect:{{0, 20}, {768, 44}}
   ▶ UIAToolbar: rect:{{0, 980}, {768, 44}}
```

Figure 35—Finding the popover element

06-Universal/step03/automation/sandbox.js
```
"use strict";

var target = UIATarget.localTarget();
var window = target.frontMostApp().mainWindow();
➤ var popover = window.popover();
➤ var tableView = popover.tableViews()[0];
var cell = tableView.cells()["coffee"];
cell.tap();
```

We're asking the window for a popover element using the popover() method that is available on any UIAElement subtype. Once we have the popover, we ask it for the first table view. Now when we run this we see the cell get tapped, the popover slide out of the way, and the map do its thing to search the nearby area.

So, we know we'll have to adapt our SearchTermScreen object to account for the popover when testing on the iPad in portrait. But what happens in landscape? Let's change the device orientation and log a window's element tree again:

06-Universal/step04/automation/sandbox.js
```
"use strict";

var target = UIATarget.localTarget();
➤ target.setDeviceOrientation(UIA_DEVICE_ORIENTATION_LANDSCAPELEFT);
➤ target.delay(1);
var window = target.frontMostApp().mainWindow();
window.logElementTree();
```

We're using the setDeviceOrientation() method on the UIATarget instance to rotate the simulator to landscape orientation using a constant.

The UI Automation documentation lists several constants you can use for all kinds of orientations, like UIA_DEVICE_ORIENTATION_PORTRAIT_UPSIDEDOWN and even UIA_DEVICE_ORIENTATION_FACEDOWN.

We also have to pause for a moment to give the rotation animation time to complete before we grab the window and log the element tree. Remember that logging the element tree happens immediately. Since we're not using one of the system query methods that polls with the timeout, we need to add a manual delay.

Press ⌘-R to stop, and press it again to restart the app and run the script. Now we see an element tree that looks like the following figure. There's no popover to be found! Instead we see *two* sets of navigation bars and toolbars as siblings within the window element—one set for the master view controller on the left, and the other for the detail view controller on the right.

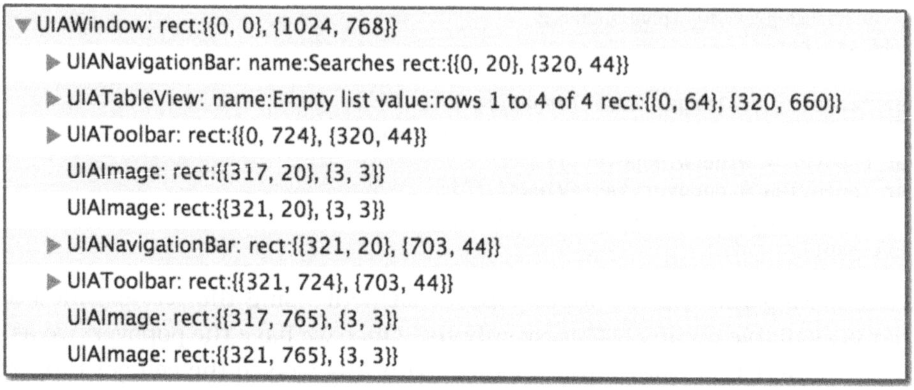

```
▼ UIAWindow: rect:{{0, 0}, {1024, 768}}
  ▶ UIANavigationBar: name:Searches rect:{{0, 20}, {320, 44}}
  ▶ UIATableView: name:Empty list value:rows 1 to 4 of 4 rect:{{0, 64}, {320, 660}}
  ▶ UIAToolbar: rect:{{0, 724}, {320, 44}}
    UIAImage: rect:{{317, 20}, {3, 3}}
    UIAImage: rect:{{321, 20}, {3, 3}}
  ▶ UIANavigationBar: rect:{{321, 20}, {703, 44}}
  ▶ UIAToolbar: rect:{{321, 724}, {703, 44}}
    UIAImage: rect:{{317, 765}, {3, 3}}
    UIAImage: rect:{{321, 765}, {3, 3}}
```

Figure 36—Element tree in landscape orientation

To users, this makes sense. That's what they see on the screen, after all. To developers like us who know the view hierarchy behind the scenes, this seems odd. Yet Apple chose to have the landscape split view controller present all these elements as siblings, most likely because of the way VoiceOver reads the screen through the accessibility APIs. You can review what we covered in Section 5.2, *Identifying Elements with Accessibility APIs*, on page 64, for more information on how that works.

Regardless, this uncovers two challenges: not only do we need to take the device family into account, but the orientation will also change how we traverse the element tree.

6.3 Building an iPad Test Suite with Reusable Pieces

We've seen how the element tree can vary on the iPad in different orientations. Now we want to apply that knowledge to our test scripts. How much can we reuse? What should we separate?

Because the interfaces are so different between the devices, it is best to make a separate test-suite file for the iPad. We can then pull in the screen objects one by one to figure out what can be reused. Here we're going to write scripts to detect the device model and orientation and then use these to help the SearchTermScreen object find the elements it needs to do its job.

Finding the Device Model

The UIATarget instance provides the model() method that returns a string describing what kind of system the app is running on. Let's run this small script to see what it returns for us now:

```
06-Universal/step05/automation/sandbox.js
var target = UIATarget.localTarget();
➤ UIALogger.logMessage(target.model());
```

In our case, we see iPad Simulator. Let's write up a quick script to test for this by using a JavaScript substring search:

```
06-Universal/step06/automation/sandbox.js
var target = UIATarget.localTarget();
if (target.model().match("iPad")) {
    UIALogger.logMessage("Running on iPad");
} else {
    UIALogger.logMessage("Running on iPhone/iPod Touch");
}
```

The match() method will return true if the string contains iPad. Since we'll be testing for this condition a lot we should pull it out into a reusable function, but where do we put it? If it were a tool that affected our test environment, then we could put it in the global namespace alongside test(), log(), and all the rest. If this affected a portion of the screen, we could put it in the appropriate screen object. Instead, this kind of method relates more to the application as a whole. So, let's create an object that reflects that and put it in lib/App.js:

```
06-Universal/step07/automation/lib/App.js
"use strict";

var App = {
    isOnIPad: function() {
        return this.target().model().match("iPad");
    },

    target: function() {
        return UIATarget.localTarget();
    }
};
```

For those of you who have strong opinions on how to camel-case the iDevice names, please cut me some slack as I name this function, isOnIPad(). I spent way too long trying to decide how to do it. Substitute your own treatment to taste.

To use this new object, we need to import the App.js file in our test-environment file so it is available everywhere we need it:

06-Universal/step07/automation/env.js
```
#import "lib/App.js";
```

We'll use this App object as a nice namespace to keep our application-level concerns separate from our other tools. In this case, it's as if we're asking the application, "Are you running on the iPad?"

Testing in Landscape Orientation

Now that we have a way to determine the device family, we are ready to start forking test code in strategic places. In an ideal world, it would be great to run a single test suite that adapts itself completely to any idiom. In practice, the iPad interface is so unique that we benefit from building a separate test suite composed of common pieces instead.

Let's create a new script file named automation/test_suite_ipad.js that imports our test environment so we have all the tools and shortcuts we started building in Chapter 4, *Organizing Test Code*, on page 41:

06-Universal/step08/automation/test_suite_ipad.js
```
"use strict";
#import "env.js";
if (!App.isOnIPad()) {
    throw new Error("Test suite only works on iPad");
}
```

As a courtesy to ourselves, we're also adding a quick conditional check that throws an error if this suite isn't run against an iPad. Now let's write a test that removes and then replaces the "coffee" search term in landscape orientation:

06-Universal/step08/automation/test_suite_ipad.js
```
test("Removing and replacing search term in landscape", function() {
    App.rotateLandscape();
    var s = SearchTermScreen;
    s.removeTerm("coffee");
    s.assertNoTerm("coffee");
    s.addTerm('coffee');
    s.assertTerm(0, 'coffee');
});
```

Previously, we had this broken out into two separate behavior tests when we experimented with building this up for the iPhone. In practice, you can mix and match your test steps any way that makes sense to you. In our case, this is just how the iPhone tests emerged. Since we're at a different starting point with the iPad, let's combine the removing and replacing behavior into one test since it represents a complete thought that puts the application back in the starting state.

We're testing landscape orientation first because we know the element tree is close enough to the iPhone version that this test should pass. The SearchTermScreen object looks for the first navigation bar and table view in the window to do its work. It should have no trouble navigating the split view controller in landscape orientation.

Note the call to the App.rotateLandscape() method. We haven't written that yet, so let's do so now:

06-Universal/step08/automation/lib/App.js
```
var App = {
    // ...
    rotateLandscape: function() {
        var orientation = UIA_DEVICE_ORIENTATION_LANDSCAPELEFT;
        this.target().setDeviceOrientation(orientation);
    },
    // ...
};
```

This gives us a meaningful yet terse way to rotate the device to the other orientation that we need to support.

Run the test suite; it passes. There's nothing like a quick and easy win to pump up our motivation before we climb the challenging hill.

Testing in Portrait Orientation

Things get tricky when we want to test in portrait orientation. Add this script to the end of the test-suite file we just started to see what happens:

06-Universal/step09/automation/test_suite_ipad.js
```
test("Removing and replacing search term in portrait", function() {
    App.rotatePortrait();
    var s = SearchTermScreen;
    s.removeTerm("coffee");
    s.assertNoTerm("coffee");
    s.addTerm('coffee');
    s.assertTerm(0, 'coffee');
});
```

It's almost exactly the same code as the other test, but instead we're starting in portrait orientation. This is an example where some code duplication can be useful. We've pulled the actual steps for removing, adding, and asserting search terms into the SearchTermScreen object and given them meaningful names. Repeating these names here helps us understand what we're actually testing while giving us the ability to reuse test code. Of course, you can take test-code reuse too far, but you get the point. Readability is the guiding factor, and deciding between duplication and extraction for reuse is a pragmatic matter.

Before we run this, we need to implement the method on the App object to rotate to portrait orientation:

```
06-Universal/step09/automation/lib/App.js
var App = {
    // ...
    rotatePortrait: function() {
        var orientation = UIA_DEVICE_ORIENTATION_PORTRAIT;
        this.target().setDeviceOrientation(orientation);
    },
    // ...
};
```

When run, we're greeted with a passing first test and a failing second test, as we expect. Our SearchTermScreen object doesn't yet know about the popover element. Let's fix that.

Adapting Screen Objects to New Idioms

We have a series of changes to make to fix our SearchTermScreen object so it works in portrait orientation. Let's look at the first point of failure in our removeTerm() method:

```
06-Universal/step09/automation/lib/screens/SearchTermScreen.js
// ...
removeTerm: function(name) {
    log("Removing search term", name);
    var editButton = this.navigationBar().leftButton();
    editButton.tap();
    var tableView = this.window().tableViews()[0];
    var cell = tableView.cells()[name];
    var deleteSwitch = cell.switches()[0];
    deleteSwitch.tap();
    var deleteButton = cell.buttons()[0];
    deleteButton.tap();
    editButton.tap();
},
// ...
```

The failure happens when we try to call this.navigationBar(), which has the Screen prototype fetch the navigation bar for us. We need to change how we fetch the navigation bar. Thanks to the JavaScript object model, we can override the navigationBar() method only in the SearchTermScreen object:

06-Universal/step10/automation/lib/screens/SearchTermScreen.js
```
navigationBar: function() {
    if (App.isOnIPad()) {
        return this.window().popover().navigationBar();
    } else {
        return this.__proto__.navigationBar();
    }
}
```

Now, when we call the navigationBar() method, this local version checks to see if we're on the iPad and then fetches the navigation bar from within the window's popover element. If we're not on the iPad, we return the original value by calling navigationBar() on the prototype, which is the JavaScript approximation of sending a message to super in Objective-C.

We have a problem, though. The landscape version of the test is now broken since we're always assuming there's a popover if running on the iPad. We need to add another method on the App object to check for orientation:

06-Universal/step11/automation/lib/App.js
```
var App = {
    // ...

    isPortrait: function() {
        var orientation = this.target().deviceOrientation();
        return orientation == UIA_DEVICE_ORIENTATION_PORTRAIT ||
            orientation == UIA_DEVICE_ORIENTATION_PORTRAIT_UPSIDEDOWN;
    },

    // ...
};
```

And now we can fix our conditional expression to look for the popover only when in portrait orientation on the iPad:

06-Universal/step11/automation/lib/screens/SearchTermScreen.js
```
➤ if (App.isOnIPad() && App.isPortrait()) {
    return this.window().popover().navigationBar();
} else {
    return this.__proto__.navigationBar();
}
```

Let's look at the rest of the removeTerm() method to see what else we may need to fix:

06-Universal/step12/automation/lib/screens/SearchTermScreen.js

```
removeTerm: function(name) {
    log("Removing search term", name);
    var editButton = this.navigationBar().leftButton();
    editButton.tap();
```

➤
```
    var tableView = this.window().tableViews()[0];
    var cell = tableView.cells()[name];

    var deleteSwitch = cell.switches()[0];
    deleteSwitch.tap();

    var deleteButton = cell.buttons()[0];
    deleteButton.tap();

    editButton.tap();
},
```

Ah, the table view. Just like the navigation bar, it's no longer a direct child of the window. We're fetching it and saving it in a local variable in several places in this screen object. This is a great time to pull it out into an instance method:

06-Universal/step13/automation/lib/screens/SearchTermScreen.js

```
tableView: function() {
    return this.window().tableViews()[0];
}
```

Now we need to change every place where we fetch the table view from the window to use this method instead:

06-Universal/step13/automation/lib/screens/SearchTermScreen.js

```
// ...
```
➤
```
var cell = this.tableView().cells()[name];

var deleteSwitch = cell.switches()[0];
deleteSwitch.tap();
// ...
```

At this point we should run the iPhone test suite against the iPhone simulator to make sure we didn't break anything. We're taking a small redesign step here by pulling out the tableView() method and checking our work. It's tempting to just plow through and make the changes we're intending to make, but taking small, executable steps is very important for a dynamically typed language like JavaScript.

Once we're confident that the test code still functions as it did before, we can augment the tableView() method to take the device and orientation into account:

06-Universal/step14/automation/lib/screens/SearchTermScreen.js
```
tableView: function() {
    var root;
    if (App.isOnIPad() && App.isPortrait()) {
        root = this.window().popover();
    } else {
        root = this.window();
    }
    return root.tableViews()[0];
}
```

This time, instead of delegating to the prototype in the else clause, we're using a variable named root to hold the root of the element tree for this screen object's elements. Sometimes it can be useful to think in terms of element subtrees. If we're in portrait orientation on the iPad, we want to find the table view element in the popover's subtree; otherwise, we want to find it in the window.

Finally, our portrait test is ready. Run it and watch both orientations pass the tests with flying colors. We've successfully adapted our reusable test-script pieces for these two tests. Run the iPhone test suite against the iPhone simulator, and we'll pass there, too.

We've walked through some steps to surgically adapt our screen objects to changes in the element tree. This is yet another advantage of grouping and organizing test steps by parts of the screen. Where appropriate, we can give these objects the intelligence they need to keep working in a variety of conditions.

Sometimes, though, we know exactly what we're looking for on the screen, and we just want a quick and dirty way to find it. Next we'll discuss how to recursively search the entire tree with predicate expressions.

6.4 Searching the Element Tree with Predicates

Up to this point, we've been giving our screen objects the intelligence to find the elements they need to get the job done. In many cases this is a great way to keep steps organized, and I recommend it. But sometimes we just want to do a quick search of the whole screen. If, say, we know there's only one button named Edit, then we don't care which toolbar it lives in.

UI Automation doesn't provide a mechanism to do this for us, but we can build our own tool using the knowledge we've gained up to this point. Rather than just look up elements by name, we're going to learn about using predicate expressions that let us execute arbitrary queries. Then we'll build a breadth-first recursive search in a series of steps. By the end, we'll have another tool in our toolbox that helps us write flexible and robust test scripts.

Building Predicates the Easy Way

In Apple's world, a predicate is an expression that evaluates to a Boolean value. Predicates are used in Objective-C for validating properties on objects and filtering collections, and they play an important role in technologies like Core Data. They are built on top of the key-value coding mechanism, so any key or key path can be used in an expression.[1]

In UI Automation, we use these same expressions to filter UIAElementArray collections. Let's see this in action by using a predicate to look up a table-cell element by name. Make sure the iPad simulator is set to portrait, and empty out the sandbox script file so it contains only this:

06-Universal/step15/automation/sandbox.js
```
"use strict";

#import "env.js";

var target = UIATarget.localTarget();
var window = target.frontMostApp().mainWindow();
var popover = window.popovers()[0];
var tableView = popover.tableViews()[0];
var cells = tableView.cells();
var cell = cells.firstWithPredicate("name = 'coffee'");
cell.tap();
```

We're manually walking down the element tree to find the table view, and then we're using the firstWithPredicate(), which tells the UIAElementArray to return the first element matching the predicate expression. If no matches are found, we get back a UIAElementNil object as usual.

Most of the time we'll be building predicates on the fly, interpolating values by appending strings together. You can use either single or double quotes to represent strings in a predicate, but you need to escape them with backslashes to make sure they match and stay balanced. Otherwise we end up with this problem:

06-Universal/step16/automation/sandbox.js
```
var cells = tableView.cells();
var fakeCafe = "Jonathan's Coffee";
var cell = cells.firstWithPredicate("name = '" + fakeCafe + "'");
```

This fails with an "Unable to parse format string" error because of the extra single quote in the name we're looking for. Manually building predicates like

---

1. http://developer.apple.com/library/ios/documentation/cocoa/conceptual/KeyValueCoding/Articles/KeyValueCoding.html

this can be tedious and error prone. In Objective-C, we're able to build predicates this way:

```
NSString *term = "Jonathan's Coffee";
NSPredicate *p = [NSPredicate predicateWithFormat:@"name = %@", term];
```

The predicateWithFormat: method takes a format string and a variable number of arguments to build a well-formed expression. When replacing the %@ placeholder with strings, it properly escapes double quotes automatically.

This is such a great idea that we should build our own predicateWithFormat() function:

06-Universal/step17/automation/env.js
```
function predicateWithFormat(format) {
    var parts = format.split("%@");
    var result = [];

    result.push(parts[0]);
    for (var i = 1; i < parts.length; i++) {
        var value = arguments[i];

        if (typeof value == 'string') {
            var allQuotes = new RegExp('"', 'g');
            value = '"' + value.replace(allQuotes, '\\"') + '"';
        }

        var part = parts[i];
        result.push(value, part);
    }

    return result.join('');
}
```

We're splitting the format string at every placeholder to get an array of all the parts, looping over them, and inserting each of the arguments passed in. We first encountered the arguments special variable back in *Painless Output with a log() Function*, on page 43. Before we insert each of these arguments, we're checking to see if they are strings and escaping and wrapping with double quotes if so. We join the array of results together and, boom, out comes a predicate expression.

This function will fit well as a top-level tool right alongside the test(), assert(), and log() functions. This is such a common string manipulation that it makes sense to put it in the global namespace. We'll use it a lot.

Now that we have a predicate builder, we can find our mythical café this way:

```
06-Universal/step17/automation/sandbox.js
var cells = tableView.cells();
var term = "Jonathan's Coffee";
var fakeCafe = "Jonathan's Coffee";
var predicate = predicateWithFormat("name = %@", fakeCafe);
var cell = cells.firstWithPredicate(predicate);
```

We won't get that malformed predicate error any more because of our predicate-WithFormat() utility function. Every predicate we build is guaranteed to be well-formed.

Recursion Through the Element Tree

Now that we can build predicates with ease, let's start building a recursive searching function to evaluate the predicates at every level of the element tree. We need a place to experiment, so clear out the automation/sandbox.js file and replace the contents with the following so we have a UIAWindow instance to start from:

```
06-Universal/step18/automation/sandbox.js
"use strict";

#import "env.js";

var target = UIATarget.localTarget();
var window = target.frontMostApp().mainWindow();
```

Let's define the recursive function right here in the sandbox for now. We're going to build it up over a couple of steps and we'll move it into its proper place once we get it working right. First we want a function that takes a predicate and a starting element:

```
06-Universal/step18/automation/sandbox.js
function searchWithPredicate(predicate, startElement) {
    target.pushTimeout(0);
    var elements = startElement.elements();
    var found = elements.firstWithPredicate(predicate);
    target.popTimeout();

    if (found.isValid()) return found;

    // ...
}
```

We have to push a timeout of zero because we don't want the system to courteously wait for the element tree to update if the match fails. That is the whole point of this function, after all. We're expecting most of our queries to fail while we walk the tree.

We ask that starting element for its subelements and query the UIAElementArray for the first match of the predicate. If nothing is found, then we get a UIAElementNil result back, which we test for with the isValid() method. If we do find a match, then we return it—we're finished.

If we don't get a match it's time to loop through all the elements and perform this same search on each of *their* UIAElementArray collections, continuing down the tree:

06-Universal/step18/automation/sandbox.js
```
    // ...

    for (var i = 0; i < elements.length; i++) {
        var element = elements[i];
        found = searchWithPredicate(predicate, element);
        if (found) return found;
    }

    return null;
}
```

For each of the elements, we call searchWithPredicate() again using the same predicate, but this time passing in the new element as the root of a subtree to search. If any of these calls returns non-null, we return it and bail out immediately so it bubbles back up the stack. If we exhausted the list of elements and still haven't found anything, we return null.

Let's try this out by searching the main window for the first element with the name "coffee":

06-Universal/step18/automation/sandbox.js
```
var predicate = predicateWithFormat("name = %@", "coffee");

var cell = searchWithPredicate(predicate, window);
cell.tap();
```

By starting at the window, our recursive function travels down the tree, reaches the popover, reaches the table view, and eventually finds the cell with the name "coffee" to return up the stack.

Restoring the Timeout

Alas, by disabling the timeout while we search, we're giving up a useful feature of UI Automation. What happens if we try to query for a point of interest before the map finishes loading? Let's add this code at the end of our sandbox and see what happens when we run it:

```
06-Universal/step19/automation/sandbox.js
var predicate = predicateWithFormat("name = %@", "coffee");
var cell = searchWithPredicate(predicate, window);
cell.tap();

➤ predicate = predicateWithFormat("name = %@", "POI: Peet's Coffee and Tea");
➤ var poi = searchWithPredicate(predicate, window);
➤ poi.tap();
```

Of course, you'll want to substitute an actual point-of-interest name that you're getting back from the API. And remember that we added the POI: prefix to the identifiers used as names back in Section 5.2, *Identifying Elements with Accessibility APIs*, on page 64.

The search term is successfully tapped, but when we try to find the point of interest, we're greeted with the rather unhelpful message null is not an object. Because we disabled the timeouts, the recursive search completed long before the points of interest had a chance to show up on the map.

Not to worry, however, because we can wrap our call to the searchWithPredicate() function with our own version of timeout polling:

```
06-Universal/step20/automation/sandbox.js
var predicate = predicateWithFormat("name = %@", "coffee");
var cell = searchWithPredicate(predicate, window);
cell.tap();

➤ var timeoutInMillis = target.timeout() * 1000;
➤ var start = new Date();
➤
➤ do {
➤     var now = new Date();
➤     predicate = predicateWithFormat("name = %@", "POI: Peet's Coffee and Tea");
➤     var poi = searchWithPredicate(predicate, window);
➤     target.delay(0.1);
➤ } while(!poi && now - start < timeoutInMillis);
➤ poi.tap();
```

We grab the current timeout value and perform a do/while loop until we either find the element we're looking for or we pass the timeout. We pause for a fraction of a second with each iteration of the loop as a courtesy to our CPU. Feel free to adjust this to taste.

This is all fine and dandy, but we don't want to write out this loop every time we need to search. Let's put this inside the searchWithPredicate() function. To do that, extract the function body as it is now to an inner function that we can wrap in the timeout, like so:

```
06-Universal/step21/automation/sandbox.js
function searchWithPredicate(predicate, startElement) {

    function recursiveSearch(predicate, startElement) {
        target.pushTimeout(0);
        var elements = startElement.elements();
        var found = elements.firstWithPredicate(predicate);
        target.popTimeout();

        if (found.isValid()) return found;
        for (var i = 0; i < elements.length; i++) {
            var element = elements[i];
            found = recursiveSearch(predicate, element);
            if (found) return found;
        }
        return null;
    }

    var timeoutInMillis = target.timeout() * 1000;
    var start = new Date();
    do {
        var now = new Date();
        var found = recursiveSearch(predicate, startElement);
        target.delay(0.1);
    } while(!found && now - start < timeoutInMillis);

    return found;
}
```

The inner function, named recursiveSearch(), has its own scope and local variables and does the dirty work of actually walking the tree. By writing it this way, we've enabled the searchWithPredicate() function to call the recursive search while setting up the timeout polling for us.

While we're cleaning up the function, this is a good time to move it to the final resting place in our toolbox. Since these searches are all about what is on the screen, the Screen object is a great destination. That gives us access to the local target through our screen-object methods, too:

```
06-Universal/step22/automation/lib/screens/Screen.js
var Screen = {
    // ...
    searchWithPredicate: function(predicate, startElement) {
        var target = this.target();
        function recursiveSearch(predicate, startElement) {
            target.pushTimeout(0);
            // ...

    }
};
```

And for the cherry on top, we can add a default element to this method. That way, if we don't pass in an element to start from, the method will assume that we mean the main window:

```
06-Universal/step22/automation/lib/screens/Screen.js
searchWithPredicate: function(predicate, startElement) {
    if (!startElement) startElement = this.window();
    // ...
```

This works because all parameters are optional in JavaScript. If you don't pass an argument in, then the parameter is undefined.

Phew! We walked through quite a few steps to build this tool. Let's use it in our sandbox to tap the "coffee" search term and tap on a point of interest on the map:

```
06-Universal/step22/automation/sandbox.js
var target = UIATarget.localTarget();
var window = target.frontMostApp().mainWindow();
var predicate = predicateWithFormat("name = %@", "coffee");

var cell = Screen.searchWithPredicate(predicate);
assert(cell, "Couldn't find cell");
cell.tap();
predicate = predicateWithFormat("name = %@", "POI: Peet's Coffee and Tea");
var poi = Screen.searchWithPredicate(predicate);
assert(poi, "Couldn't find point of interest");
poi.tap();
```

To help with debugging, I've put in assert() calls to give us a more meaningful failure if we don't get an element back from our search. With all the other query methods that UI Automation provides, we get back a UIAElementNil instance that acts both as a sentinel to stop the script dead in its tracks and as a placeholder to represent what we were looking for. We cannot make one of those instances ourselves, so we're stuck returning null as the fail condition of the recursion. An assertion error message like this is sufficient.

We've learned a bit about predicates, written our own predicate builder, and set up a recursive searching function to find any element that matches. Let's take this to the next level and see how predicates can help us find any element by name *and* type.

6.5 Advanced Predicate Usage and Beyond

Now that we have the predicate basics down, let's take a moment to imagine some use cases that may not be obvious but are quite powerful. Searching for elements by name anywhere on the screen could give us false positives. Let's narrow our search by building a predicate to find the first element that matches a given name *and* type:

```
06-Universal/step23/automation/sandbox.js
var predicate = predicateWithFormat("name = %@ and class.description = %@",
                                    "coffee",
                                    "UIATableCell");
var cell = Screen.searchWithPredicate(predicate);
assert(cell, "Couldn't find cell");
cell.tap();
```

This works because of the way predicates interact with key-value coding in Objective-C. The elements that we talk to in JavaScript are actually Objective-C objects under the hood. The key path class.description accesses the element's class key and in turn accesses the class's description key. Note that we're not talking to UITableViewCell objects, but rather to the UIATableCell elements that represent them in UI Automation. Any property of an element can be used in an expression.

We're not restricted to equality checking. We already saw the beginswith operator back in Section 5.2, *Identifying Elements with Accessibility APIs*, on page 64. Since the point-of-interest pins prefix the accessibility identifiers with the string POI:, we can do a search for one of those pins without having to drill down to the map element:

```
var predicate = predicateWithFormat("name beginswith %@", "POI: Starbucks");
var pin = Screen.searchWithPredicate(predicate);
```

There's no need to specify the type of element to search for since we're using a prefix that won't exist in other element names. Custom accessibility identifiers and predicate searches offer quite a bit of flexibility. We can do case-insensitive matches, ignore diacritics, use regular expressions, and even do simple set-based operations in predicate expressions. Let this sink in for a moment. We have a lot of power here.

And of course, we also have a lot of responsibility. Just because we *can* run these recursive searches doesn't mean it's always wise. This works best when you have custom identifiers and take steps to avoid false positive matches. This recursive search is just one of our tools. Apply it thoughtfully to the problem at hand.

We've played with quite a bit of fire here. We experimented with adapting our existing tools to work well on both the iPad and iPhone. We dove deep into the power of predicates and built a breadth-first recursive search of the element tree—not to mention all the JavaScript we wrote! This has been the most challenging part of our journey so far. Well done.

Next we'll move beyond just testing behavior and use the power of UI Automation and Instruments together to test and measure performance.

CHAPTER 7

Automating Performance Tests

We've got a problem. Several users complained that NearbyMe crashes after being used for a while. We're able to reproduce the bug if we try searching for results nearby over and over again. It turns out that the watchdog process is killing our app because the memory usage keeps going up.

Performance testing isn't just a good idea—it's critical for useful and successful iOS apps. We need to guard our memory usage, launch time, and responsiveness. Otherwise, the watchdog process may decide that our app needs to be sacrificed for the good of the device and the user will give up altogether in frustration.

The problem is that performance testing can be boring. Searching for issues takes time. Once we discover a hot spot to fix we have to trigger the same actions over and over while working out a solution. Thankfully, UI Automation comes to our rescue.

We're going to track down our memory leak using Instruments, but instead of just tapping around manually each time we want to re-create the results, we're going to use UI Automation to capture our actions as a script. Once we have a way to reliably re-create the problem, we'll try to fix it and check our work with the memory benchmarks through those same captured steps. We'll also learn how to stress-test our application by triggering memory warnings and randomly touching all over the screen. By the end, you'll know how to battle-test your apps and squeeze out many of those nasty performance bugs.

7.1 Setting Up Custom Instruments Templates

We've been using Instruments's trace document templates with the out-of-the-box UI Automation template. Now we're going to create a custom template that's ready to go so we can quickly get started automating the steps performed during the memory analysis.

To begin, load up the NearbyMe project from the 07-Performance/step01 directory. Make sure Xcode is set to build for the iPhone simulator, and choose Profile from the Product menu or press ⌘-I to build and launch the app in Instruments. Choose the UI Automation template like we've done before, but this time stop the Instruments trace once the new trace document opens. We don't need the app running, because we're going to save a template of this document when we're finished.

Open the instruments library by clicking on the Library button at the top of the trace-document window in the toolbar, or press ⌘-L. We're going to keep it simple and only add the Allocations instrument for these examples. Search for the instrument by typing "allocations" in the search box at the bottom of the library window, and drag it underneath the Automation instrument in the track pane, like in the following figure.

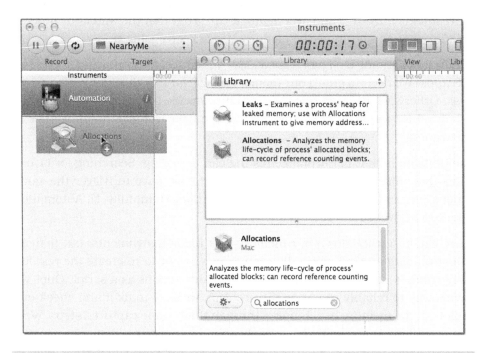

Figure 37—Adding new instruments

Now we're ready to save this as a template for quick reuse. Choose Save as Template from the File menu. Name the template Automated Allocations, click the blank icon box to choose an icon, fill in a useful description, and save it like we see in the following figure.

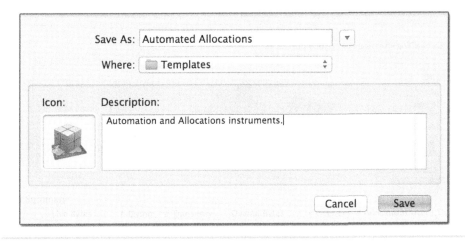

Figure 38—Saving a custom template

Let's check to make sure it works. Close Instruments and the iOS Simulator. In Xcode, press ⌘-I to build and launch the app with Instruments. Once you see the template-picker dialog window, choose All under the User section in the sidebar. Here we'll see all the templates in the default Instruments user library folder, as shown in Figure 39, *Selecting a user-generated template*, on page 104. Choose the template we just created, and a new trace document appears ready to go.

Creating templates like this is a great way to get started quickly automating common performance tests. Feel free to tweak the individual instruments' settings any way you want before saving the template file. You can even build a template with an automation script imported or embedded to execute as soon as the app launches.

Now that we've got the template ready, let's put it to use against a real, live memory leak.

7.2 Capturing Steps to Reproduce a Memory Leak

We're going to try to track down the memory leak and capture our steps with UI Automation. We want to end up with a script that we can run repeatedly while we dig into the Objective-C code to figure out where the leak might be.

We first learned about capturing automation steps back in Chapter 1, *UI Automation Overview*, on page 1. The capturing mechanism doesn't always record everything we do, but it does get us most of the way there. This helps quickly build one-off scripts while you're trying to re-create a complex problem.

Figure 39—Selecting a user-generated template

Select the UI Automation instrument in the window's track view, click the Add button in the Scripts section of the left sidebar, and choose Create to start a new blank script in the script pane.

Make sure Instruments is stopped by clicking the red record button at the upper left of the trace-document window. We want to make sure our captured automation actions walk through the application from its launch. That way we can simply press ⌘-R to start a new trace running the script, and we don't have to touch the application at all.

While we're poking around to re-create the problem, let's capture our actions like we first learned about in Section 1.1, *Capturing Our First Script from the Simulator*, on page 2. Press the capture button at the bottom of the script pane. Manually tap the "coffee" search term and wait for the map to zoom in and plot the pins. Then tap the Back button; the following figure shows the steps.

Figure 40—Stepping through the app looking for memory issues

Click the stop button at the bottom of the script pane; we see a script like this:

```
07-Performance/step01/automation/test_for_memory_leak.js
var target = UIATarget.localTarget();

target.frontMostApp().mainWindow().tableViews()[0].cells()["coffee"].tap();
target.frontMostApp().navigationBar().leftButton().tap();
```

This isn't a true recording of our steps because we paused for a moment while we waited for the map results to load. The script recorder didn't deduce this, so we'll need to type in a delay:

```
07-Performance/step02/automation/test_for_memory_leak.js
var target = UIATarget.localTarget();

target.frontMostApp().mainWindow().tableViews()[0].cells()["coffee"].tap();
target.delay(5);
target.frontMostApp().navigationBar().leftButton().tap();
```

Now press ⌘-R to start a new trace. Instruments terminates and relaunches the app to begin the trace recording. As long as Run on Record is checked in the left sidebar of the UI Automation instrument, the script will execute immediately. After the script finishes running, stop the Instruments trace by pressing ⌘-R again.

We have a script to re-create the conditions for the leak, and we've captured a trace recording of the application. Let's start analyzing the results.

Searching Through the Allocations Results

Tracking down leaks can be overwhelming, so when you have no clues it helps to start by filtering the Allocations instrument results to show only instances of classes that you own. Apple recommends using three-character prefixes on class names, and if you've followed that convention, filtering the results is pretty simple.[1] Type "NBM" in the search box in the upper-right corner of the trace document, and you'll see results similar to those in the following figure.

These filters are global and apply to the log pane for *every* instrument, even UI Automation. When you switch back to the Automation instrument, you'll want to clear the filter, or you won't see anything in the trace log!

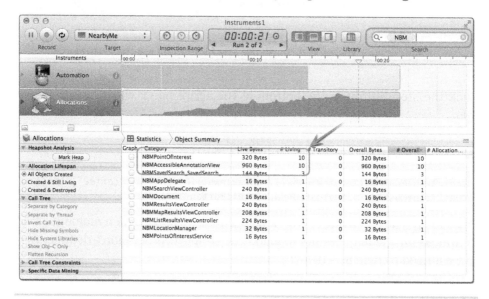

Figure 41—Finding memory problems in Instruments

---

1. http://developer.apple.com/library/ios/documentation/cocoa/conceptual/ProgrammingWithObjectiveC/Conventions/Conventions.html

Let's take a close look at the filtered results. Uh-oh. Right at the top of the list we see that the NBMAccessibleAnnotationView objects and their NBMPointOfInterest objects were still alive when we ended the trace. But our captured actions ended on the search-term screen. The results view controller and the map should have been released. Why are these objects still around?

We know these objects should be gone because of the way NearbyMe fetches and displays results. The NBMResultsViewController creates and maintains a strong reference to an NBMPointsOfInterestService class that communicates with Open-StreetMap. That instance gives us a collection of NBMPointOfInterest objects that implement the MKAnnotation protocol and are ready to add to the map. When the map wants to plot an annotation, it asks us to instantiate an annotation view, which we do with our custom NBMAccessibleAnnotationView instances.

When the results view controller is disposed of, all these points of interest and annotation views should also go away, yet here they are. It's possible that we're holding on to a strong reference that should have been a weak reference, causing a retain cycle. Let's dig a little deeper.

Fixing the Problem

Now that we've captured a script to reproduce the leak and identified classes to watch for in the Allocations instrument, let's read the Objective-C code to learn more. In Xcode, open the NBMResultsViewController and look for the property that references the NBMPointsOfInterestService API class:

07-Performance/step03/NearbyMe/NBMResultsViewController.m
```
@interface NBMResultsViewController ()

@property (strong, nonatomic) NBMPointsOfInterestService *poiService;
// ...
```

We're defining a strong property that will retain the poiService object. That makes sense because the service needs to be kept around while the network calls are made before passing back the results. This view controller is responsible for this particular service-object instance. When we instantiate the service object, we retain it in this strong property and then assign ourselves as the delegate like so:

07-Performance/step03/NearbyMe/NBMResultsViewController.m
```
self.poiService = [NBMPointsOfInterestService service];
self.poiService.delegate = self;
```

This kind of delegate relationship is quite common in Apple's world. Objects are *supposed* to hold weak references to their delegates because an object doesn't own its delegate. Using strong references for delegate properties is a pretty common mistake. Let's check out the NBMPointsOfInterestService class definition to see how the delegate property is defined:

07-Performance/step03/NearbyMe/NBMPointsOfInterestService.h
```
@interface NBMPointsOfInterestService : NSObject
```
➤ ```
@property (strong, nonatomic) id<NBMPointsOfInterestServiceDelegate> delegate;
```
```
// ...
```

Aha—this could be the problem! We've committed the sin of making a delegate property a strong reference. Our results view controller retains this service instance, which retains the results view controller. Both of their retain counts will be greater than one, and they will never be released unless we were to manually break the cycle by setting one of these properties to nil.

We need to change this property to a weak reference. That way, the retain count of the results view controller won't increase when assigned as the delegate:

07-Performance/step04/NearbyMe/NBMPointsOfInterestService.h
```
@interface NBMPointsOfInterestService : NSObject
```
➤ ```
@property (weak, nonatomic) id<NBMPointsOfInterestServiceDelegate> delegate;
```
```
// ...
```

There's a pretty good chance we've solved the problem. Let's build and run our automation script to see the results. In Xcode, press ⌘-I to build and send the app over Instruments. Instruments will keep our trace document loaded and we can press ⌘-R to launch the app and automate the steps. Once the script finishes, inspect the results in Figure 42, *We've squashed the memory leak*, on page 109.

Success! We can see that the NBMPointOfInterest and NBMAccessibleAnnotationView objects are gone. After returning to the search-term list, all the objects related to the results view controller are released, just as we expect. In the track view of the Allocations instrument, we see the memory footprint drop dramatically after we fixed the bug—more evidence that we did the right thing.

If the bug were hidden deeper, we could keep walking through the same steps, changing Objective-C code, building and profiling in Instruments, and running the script to re-create the results. Getting in this groove is critical since it removes the need to interact with the app at all.

Just remember that the search filter we applied to the trace document applies to *every* instrument we're looking at. If you want to switch back to the

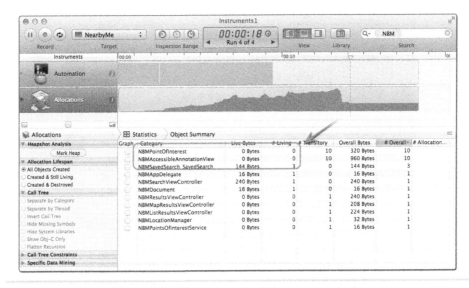

Figure 42—We've squashed the memory leak.

Automation instrument to check the trace log, make sure you remove the "NBM" from the search bar at the top of the window, or you won't see anything in the log!

Next let's take our memory bug–hunting skills to another level and look at a technique to trigger memory warnings in the simulator.

7.3 Triggering Simulator Memory Warnings with AppleScript

Since we are testing memory footprint, it would be great if we could trigger memory warnings in iOS Simulator from our scripts. When an iOS application receives a memory warning, Apple says any cached data that can be easily re-created should be discarded. This is often a source of latent bugs because we're either not disposing of this cached information like we should, or we dispose of cached information that is still in use.

Memory warnings are triggered manually within iOS Simulator by choosing Simulate Memory Warning from the Hardware menu, like we see in Figure 43, *Simulating a memory warning*, on page 110. Thanks to some AppleScript magic and the UIAHost object, we can trigger these at any point we want from our script files.

We're going to build this functionality in two steps. First we need to write the AppleScript that triggers the menu item. Then we'll build the scripts we need in UI Automation to trigger the action.

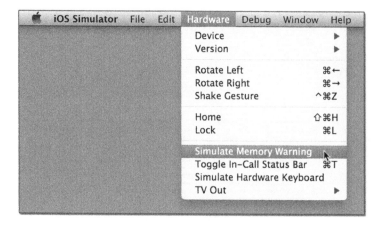

Figure 43—Simulating a memory warning

Building AppleScripts to Control Mac Applications

AppleScript uses the same mechanisms as VoiceOver and other assistive technologies to manipulate the UI, which means we must enable this access to the user interface in OS X. Turn this on by going to the System Preferences app, viewing the Accessibility preference pane, and checking the "Enable access for assistive devices" check box, as shown in Figure 44, *Turn on AppleScript's ability to select menus*, on page 111.

Now we need an AppleScript that lets us choose the menu item to simulate a memory warning. Load up the built-in AppleScript Editor in the /Applications/Utilities directory. This is a great tool that lets us try out script snippets on the fly to see how they work.

After a bit of trial and error, I figured out that the proper AppleScript to find menu items in the simulator looks like this:

07-Performance/step05/controlling_simulator.applescript
```
tell application "System Events" ¬
    to click menu item "Simulate Memory Warning" ¬
    of menu "Hardware" ¬
    of menu bar item "Hardware" ¬
    of menu bar 1 ¬
    of process "iPhone Simulator"
```

We instruct the System Events process to send click events directly to the iPhone simulator. We're writing this command as one long line with breaks because this makes it easier for us to invoke from the UIAHost instance, which

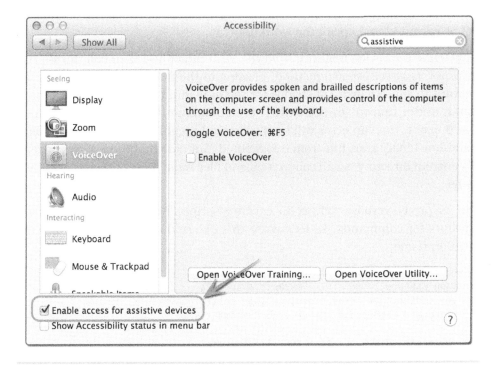

Figure 44—Turn on AppleScript's ability to select menus.

we'll get to in a moment. Those line breaks can be typed into the AppleScript Editor by pressing ⌥-↵.

We're not going much deeper into AppleScript in this book. We just need enough to trigger this menu item. For more information, check out *Apple Training Series: AppleScript 1-2-3 [Sog09]*.

Calling External Scripts from Within UI Automation

We can run AppleScript snippets with the osascript command-line tool, but how do we trigger that from our automation script? The UIAHost object is the only window to the world outside of Instruments and our application. It provides a method that lets us execute any Unix command on the host Mac running the simulator. Let's try it out by triggering the say command to listen to the machine talk. Switch back to Instruments, create a new embedded automation script, and type this into the script pane:

```
07-Performance/step06/automation/sandbox.js
var target = UIATarget.localTarget();
var host = target.host();
host.performTaskWithPathArgumentsTimeout("/usr/bin/say", ["Hello"], 5);
```

Make sure the volume is up on your Mac when you run it. The say command will be executed and speak the word Hello.

We retrieve the UIAHost instance from the local target and then call the performTaskWithPathArgumentsTimeout() method, passing in the full path to the command we want to run, an array of strings for the individual arguments to the command, and a timeout in seconds. If the command doesn't complete before that timeout, then an error will be thrown and recorded in the log. Any command-line binary runs fine from this method, but note that there is no concept of a current directory, so all commands and files must be specified as absolute paths.

This is pretty verbose syntax to execute scripts. We don't need different timeouts for commands, so let's wrap this external interaction in a shorter function name:

```
07-Performance/step07/automation/sandbox.js
function execute() {          // variable arguments
    var cmdString = Array.prototype.join.call(arguments, " ");
    UIALogger.logMessage("Executing: " + cmdString);

    var host = UIATarget.localTarget().host();
    var cmd = arguments[0];
    var args = Array.prototype.slice.call(arguments, 1);
    var result = host.performTaskWithPathArgumentsTimeout(cmd, args, 5);

    if (result.exitCode > 0) {
        UIALogger.logError(result.stdout);
        UIALogger.logError(result.stderr);
    }
    return result;
}
execute("/usr/bin/say", "Hello");
```

We execute the same say command as before, but this time using the variable-argument magic that we first covered in *Painless Output with a log() Function*, on page 43. The first argument to the function will always be assumed to be the executable name, and all the other arguments after that will be passed along as string arguments to the command. We're also always assuming a five-second timeout, which is fine for what we're doing here. Feel free to adjust that as needed for your own tests.

To help with debugging, we inspect the result object returned from the performTaskWithPathArgumentsTimeout() method. That object has three useful properties. The exitCode is the integer exit status code returned by the command itself. Any value greater than zero means there was a problem. If the command fails, then we're logging the command's output as an error so we can review the problems in the trace logs. The stdout and stderr properties correspond to the output received from the command to standard out and standard error, respectively. At the end, we return this result object to the caller just in case there's any more processing that should be done after an error.

Now that we have a simple function to execute arbitrary system commands, we're ready to execute the AppleScript snippet to trigger the memory warning. Run it with the osascript command like so:

07-Performance/step08/automation/sandbox.js

```
var cmd = 'tell application "System Events" ' +
        'to click menu item "Simulate Memory Warning" ' +
        'of menu "Hardware" of menu bar item "Hardware" ' +
        'of menu bar 1 of process "iPhone Simulator"';
execute("/usr/bin/osascript", "-e", cmd);
```

We build up the single line of AppleScript one chunk at a time by concatenating it. Then we pass that along to our execute() function as the second parameter to /usr/bin/osascript.

Now that we've proven out the idea, we should move this execute() function to live alongside log() and test() and all the other top-level functions in our env.js file. Now let's build another function that we can call any time we want to trigger a memory warning in the simulator:

07-Performance/step09/automation/env.js

```
function triggerMemoryWarning() {
    if (!UIATarget.localTarget().model().match("Simulator")) {
        log("Can't trigger memory warnings on device");
        return;
    }
    var cmd = 'tell application "System Events" ' +
            'to click menu item "Simulate Memory Warning" ' +
            'of menu "Hardware" of menu bar item "Hardware" ' +
            'of menu bar 1 of process "iPhone Simulator"';
    var result = execute("/usr/bin/osascript", "-e", cmd);
    if (result.exitCode > 0) {
        UIALogger.logError("Could not trigger memory warning");
    } else {
        UIALogger.logWarning("Triggered memory warning");
    }
}
```

First, we perform a quick check to see if the test is running against the simulator. Triggering memory warnings with our AppleScript works only on the simulator, so if our test is running against a device, then this function returns silently.

We grab the result after we execute the AppleScript and check the exit status code. If it didn't succeed, we log an error explaining what we were attempting to do. If it did succeed, then we use UIALogger.logWarning() as a way to flag that an important event occurred during the course of the test script. These "warning" log types are really useful because they show up as orange in the Automation instrument timeline. That way we can see exactly when a memory warning was triggered while we study other instruments in the trace document.

Now that we can trigger memory warnings in the simulator from within our test scripts, let's use this as part of our arsenal to attack our application and watch it under stress.

7.4 Stress Testing

The power of Instruments really shines when you're trying to stress-test. Multithreaded applications running under resource constraints are very complicated to debug. As we've discussed, memory warnings can trigger at any moment and the application needs to be ready to handle them. What if something was purged that the app needed? What if two simultaneous operations conflict or one completes later than expected?

Testing iOS applications isn't just about testing behavior or hunting for specific performance issues. It also means stress-testing to expose race conditions or other strange bugs that surface under heavy load. Users may not walk through the same outrageous steps as your stress tests, but they may encounter some of the same cases that come up. Stress tests significantly increase the opportunity for error, increasing the chance that you'll discover annoying or even catastrophic bugs.

We're going to try a couple of ways to stress-test NearbyMe. We'll use a repetitive approach and watch the app execute the same sequence of steps over and over. Then we'll use an open source script to randomly pound events into the app so we can see what happens to it.

Performing the Same Steps Over and Over

Earlier, we used capture and playback to record simple steps to reproduce a problem. Rather than do that again here, we're going to reuse the JavaScript testing toolbox we've been building. The user's behavior steps are already encoded in our screen objects; let's use them!

For this stress test, let's tap a search term and then quickly tap the Back button thirty times. It's possible that a user may tap on the wrong search term on accident and want to quickly go back to try again. Let's mimic that behavior to the extreme with this test in automation/stress_test.js:

```
07-Performance/step10/automation/stress_test.js
"use strict";
#import "env.js";
for (var i = 0; i < 30; i++) {
    test("View map and go back, iteration: " + i, function() {
        SearchTermScreen.tapTerm("coffee");
        ResultsScreen.goBack();
        if (i % 4 == 0) triggerMemoryWarning();
    });
}
```

We're using a simple JavaScript for loop to iterate over and over. Each time we are declaring a test group that uses our screen objects to tap the "coffee" search term and immediately go back. To keep the app on its toes, we're also triggering a memory warning every fourth time.

Run the script by pressing ⌘-R twice to stop and restart the Instruments trace; we get a result like Figure 45, *Instruments results for repetitive stress testing*, on page 116.

We can see the orange regions in the Automation timeline where we logged the memory warnings. We can tell at a glance in the Allocations timeline that we're cleaning up after ourselves. The rapid activity-switching between view controllers looks okay so far.

Repetition is just one way to stress-test an app. Let's try a bit of randomness to spice things up!

Chaos Testing with UI AutoMonkey

Sometimes you don't know what you want to stress-test. You'd just like to see what "butt dialing" does to the app. UI Automation can help with that, too. It's such a useful technique to discover crashes and leaks that I built a script that does most of the work for you.

Allow me to introduce the UI AutoMonkey.[2] It's a script file for UI Automation that is inspired by Chaos Monkey, a tool Netflix built to hammer its network infrastructure, looking for weak points.[3] AutoMonkey does the same thing, but for iOS applications. It's kinda fun to watch the fruit of your hard labor wilt under the strain—consider it a form of personal stress relief.

---

2. https://github.com/jonathanpenn/ui-auto-monkey
3. http://techblog.netflix.com/2012/07/chaos-monkey-released-into-wild.html

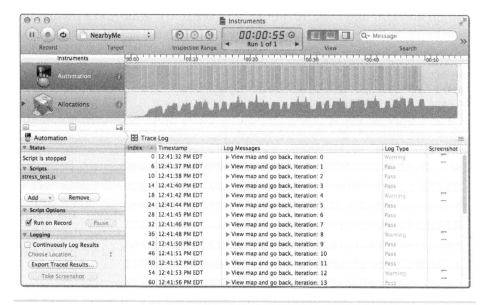

Figure 45—Instruments results for repetitive stress testing

Out of the box, the script will run for 1,000 iterations, tapping everywhere on the screen, dragging and flicking, rotating, and even locking and unlocking the device at random. You configure the probabilities by adjusting a set of configuration dictionaries at the top of the UIAutoMonkey object:

07-Performance/step11/automation/UIAutoMonkey.js
```
config: {
    numberOfEvents: 1000,
    delayBetweenEvents: 0.05,    // In seconds
    // Events are triggered based on the relative weights here. The event
    // with this highest number gets triggered the most.
    //
    // If you want to add your own "events", check out the event method
    // definitions below.
    eventWeights: {
        tap: 500,
        drag: 1,
        flick: 1,
        orientation: 1,
        clickVolumeUp: 1,
        clickVolumeDown: 1,
        lock: 1,
        pinchClose: 10,
        pinchOpen: 10,
        shake: 1
    },
```

```
    // Probability that touch events will have these different properties
    touchProbability: {
        multipleTaps: 0.05,
        multipleTouches: 0.05,
        longPress: 0.05
    }
    // ...
```

For each iteration the monkey checks the config.eventWeights setting to choose
which event to fire next. The numbers express the relative probability that
any of those events will happen. For touch events, there is also a config.touch-
Probability dictionary to decide if it should use multiple taps with multiple fingers
or a long press.

It's pretty simple to add your own events. In fact, let's add an event to trigger
a memory warning every so often. All we have to do is add a new key at the
end of the eventWeights dictionary like so:

07-Performance/step12/automation/UIAutoMonkey.js
```
eventWeights: {
    tap: 500,
    drag: 1,
    flick: 1,
    // ...
    shake: 1,
➤    memoryWarning: 50
},
```

That sets up the memoryWarning event to be one-tenth as likely to happen as
the tap event.

Once that is in place, we need to add a special method farther down in the
object. Every one of these event names has a corresponding Event method
on the UIAutoMonkey object. Since we added memoryWarning, let's add a memory-
WarningEvent() method after the shakeEvent() method, like so:

07-Performance/step12/automation/UIAutoMonkey.js
```
shakeEvent: function() {
    this.target().shake();
},
➤ memoryWarningEvent: function() {
➤     triggerMemoryWarning();
➤ },
```

When it's time for this event, we call the triggerMemoryWarning() function we wrote
earlier. Since UI AutoMonkey was built to be standalone; it doesn't know
about our JavaScript toolbox unless we import it, so we need to import env.js
at the top of the UIAutoMonkey.js file:

07-Performance/step12/automation/UIAutoMonkey.js

```
#import "env.js";

var UIAutoMonkey = {

    // ...
```

Let's try it out by profiling NearbyMe in Instruments with our custom template. Load the UIAutoMonkey.js file and run it against the application.

While it's going, we see something similar to the following figure. Our poor, poor application is really under a lot of stress now!

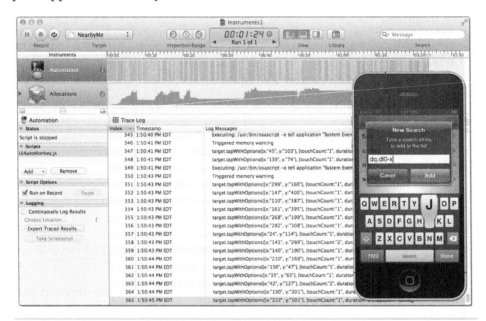

Figure 46—UI AutoMonkey in action

This isn't as surgical as the planned testing we've been writing up to this point. Chaos testing puts tremendous pressure on the application in ways a user never would, but the point is to increase the likelihood that a race condition or other latent bug shows up before we ship. I've found all sorts of bugs in my application and even Apple's frameworks using this technique.

Interpreting the Results

So, we have two stress-testing techniques, repetitive and chaos. How do we know what we're looking for in the results? Alas, performance tuning requires more than just some general recipes for success. Quite a bit depends on how an application's architecture is laid out. In some cases, like dealing with large images, we need to be very careful about memory usage since we can consume our allotment very quickly. For other types of small data, it may not matter. Keeping caches around is important for speed, but it also uses memory. There are always trade-offs.

Two tactics help. First, know your tools. Study up on how Instruments works and how you can use it to evaluate your applications. I recommend that you check out the Instruments tutorials in the Apple's World Wide Developer Conference videos, and read the book *Advanced Mac OS X Programming: The Big Nerd Ranch Guide [Dal11].*[4] You can monitor CPU usage, Core Data activity, and even trace graphics performance on a real device. By studying Instruments, you'll be able to better understand what you should look for and the kinds of performance tests to write.

Second, keep your trace logs around as historical benchmarks. You can save your trace document for later and add a new trace run to see if you've made a dent. At the top of the Instruments window you'll see arrow buttons like in the following figure. Click those buttons to step back through all the trace recordings of this document. The automation scripts help you re-create the problem with the exact same steps. It's a powerful way to watch performance characteristics over time.

Figure 47—Reviewing past results

We've used the power of Instruments to find and squash a memory leak. By capturing scripts on the fly we experiment with different user behaviors until we know what steps trigger problems. By using the testing toolbox we've been growing over the course of this book, we write repetitive tests quickly and watch our application under stress.

Next let's learn how to seed iOS applications with data when they launch—giving our tests the consistent results that they need.

---

4.   https://developer.apple.com/videos/

CHAPTER 8

Setting Up Application Data

All along we've had to manually make sure NearbyMe starts in the right state for our tests. If we removed a search term, we had to make sure to put it back. This is, unfortunately, fragile. Instead, we want a way to tell our app to launch with a consistent set of data for our tests.

But more than that, we need customized sets of data for different kinds of tests. NearbyMe uses table-view animations to shuffle the search terms around when you switch the sorting order from alphabetical to recently used. We've never even checked to see how well it performs with a large number of table cells. These problems require prefabricated application data, and that's what we're going to cover next.

We'll begin by talking a bit about how we can install application data packages into the app sandbox when installing from Xcode. Then we'll see how to dynamically generate whatever data we need in Objective-C code with a data factory. We'll command and control that data factory at app launch with bootstrap code that responds to environment variables. And finally, we'll cover how to hide test-related code from release using conditional compilation and separate build targets. Using these techniques, you'll be able to set up data for whatever you need in your own applications.

8.1 Seeding Data in Xcode with Application Data Packages

For our first technique, we're going to use a feature of Xcode schemes that lets us specify an *application data package* to load into the simulator or device alongside the app when built and run from the Xcode GUI. This package completely replaces whatever is in the application's sandbox, effectively resetting documents and preferences. You can pull these packages off live devices, so it's a great way to take a snapshot of state you want to save for later.

To learn this technique, we'll write a behavior test for the sorting in NearbyMe that depends on a specific set of search terms. We'll first create an application data package that we'll use as a baseline. We'll store this data package in our project repository and set up a testing scheme that installs it along with the application when launched from Xcode. Finally, we'll write a UI Automation behavior test that starts with this application state and checks to make sure toggling the sort order works as expected.

Downloading a Data Package from a Device

Let's set up our app the way we'll need it when we write our sorting test. Build and run NearbyMe on your iOS device and empty out the table view of search terms after it launches. Add a new set of search terms manually by entering them in this order: apple, orange, banana, and kiwi. The application adds new search terms to the top of the list, which means the final order you see on the screen should be kiwi, banana, orange, apple, like in the following figure. Toggling the sort buttons at the bottom of the screen should shuffle these between alphabetical and recent order. We'll verify this reordering in our test.

Figure 48—Adding terms for a sort-order behavior test

Now we're ready to download the data. Open the Xcode Organizer by choosing Organizer from the Window menu. Make sure the Devices tab is selected, find your iOS device in the sidebar, and click on the Applications section like we see in the following figure. Search for NearbyMe in the list of installed applications. When selected, you'll see the app sandbox file structure in the bottom window pane.

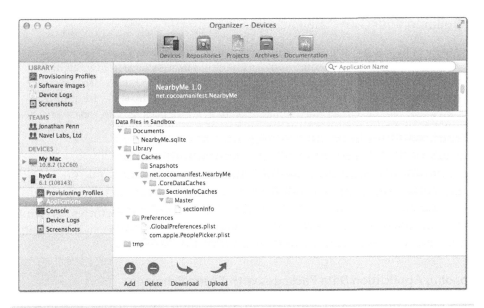

Figure 49—Viewing application data on a device

From here, click the Download button in the bottom bar of the window and save the result to someplace easily reached, like the Desktop. It saves as an .xcappdata package, a directory that OS X treats like a file.

Right-click on the package file and choose Show Package Contents. A Finder window opens showing the same directory structure that we saw in the Xcode Organizer window (see the following figure).

Figure 50—Contents of the application data package

The AppDataInfo.plist is just a file with metadata describing where the package came from. The rest of the directory structure is an exact copy of the application sandbox that was on the device. If we use this package, everything in here will be copied over to the simulator or device when installed and run in the Xcode GUI.

Building Your Own Data Packages

You don't have to go through the rigmarole to download live packages for later use if you know exactly what you want. You can build your own package from scratch. Just match the directory structure you see in these examples. You don't need to create the AppDataInfo.plist metadata file. Once you rename the enclosing folder with the .xcappdata extension, the Finder will automatically treat it as a package and you can reference it from Xcode.

For our purposes, we don't need anything except the database file. Since we're going to keep this data package with our project for the long term, let's clean it out by removing the AppDataInfo.plist and all the extra directories. We only need the AppData/Documents/NearbyMe.sqlite file. Rename the package to SortTestData.xcappdata to reflect what it will be used for.

Loading Application Data Packages with Xcode Schemes

Now we can instruct Xcode to load our application data package in a custom Xcode testing scheme. Drag the SortTestData.xcappdata file into the Xcode workspace sidebar and check the box so Xcode copies it into the workspace directory like we see in the following figure.

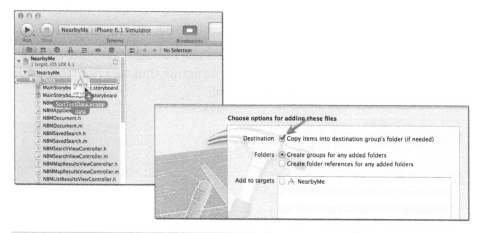

Figure 51—Copy an application data package to Xcode.

Create a new test-specific scheme by choosing Product > Scheme > Manage Schemes to bring up the list of schemes in the project. Copy the NearbyMe scheme by choosing Duplicate from the pop-up menu seen in step 1 of the following figure. Change the name of the new scheme to NearbyMeUITests and choose the data package as shown in step 2. Once you click OK, make sure you check the Shared check box for the new scheme, as seen in step 3. This makes sure that the scheme is shared and committed in your source control. If you work on a team or use continuous-integration build servers, you'll want this scheme available everywhere.

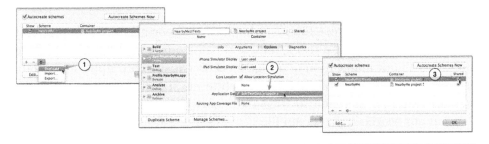

Figure 52—Creating a new test-specific scheme with the data package

This scheme *will wipe out existing app data when run from Xcode.* Let's use it and make sure it works. Choose the scheme by selecting it from the active scheme picker in the upper-left corner of Xcode, as in the following figure.

Figure 53—Use the new test-specific scheme.

Build and run in the simulator. Try adding or deleting some search terms. If you reinstall the app with Xcode, you'll see everything put back just the way it was in our data package!

Testing the Sort Ordering

Now we're finally ready to write our sort-ordering test. We'll breeze through the test code quickly using the environment we started building in Chapter 4, *Organizing Test Code*, on page 41. Create a new automation-test file in the project named automation/test_sorting.js with these contents:

08-AppData/step01/automation/test_sorting.js

```
"use strict";
#import "env.js";
test("Test search term sorting", function() {
    var s = SearchTermScreen;
    s.sortByRecent();
    s.assertSearchTermOrder(["kiwi", "banana", "orange", "apple"]);
    s.sortByName();
    s.assertSearchTermOrder(["apple", "banana", "kiwi", "orange"]);
});
```

We're starting a new test file in strict mode, importing our reusable test environment, specifying a test group, and using our SearchTermScreen object to interact with our application at a high level. Because of our application data package, we know exactly what the search terms should be when sorted. We need to write the methods to trigger the sort-button changes, so let's put those in our search-term screen file:

08-AppData/step01/automation/lib/screens/SearchTermScreen.js

```
sortByRecent: function() {
    log("Sorting search terms by recent");
    this.toolbar().segmentedControls()[0].buttons()[0].tap();
},
sortByName: function() {
    log("Sorting search terms by name");
    this.toolbar().segmentedControls()[0].buttons()[1].tap();
},
```

There's nothing revolutionary here. We're simply finding the segmented control in the toolbar and tapping the appropriate buttons. Notice that we're using the numeric index instead of the name. We could use the visible button names to find them, but those would need to be localized and our test would break in different languages. We could set the accessibilityIdentifier of the buttons in our code so they are consistent regardless of localization, like we saw in Chapter 5, *Maps, Gestures, and Alerts*, on page 59, but using the numeric index is just fine for these tests. If the index needed to change because of new features, we'd only have to change the index references in this one file to keep our tests in sync. Now we're ready to write the high-level assertion for sort order on our SearchTermScreen object:

08-AppData/step01/automation/lib/screens/SearchTermScreen.js

```
assertSearchTermOrder: function(terms) {
    var termCells = this.tableView().cells().toArray();
    var actualTerms = termCells.map(function(cell) {
        return cell.name();
    });
    assertEqualArrays(actualTerms, terms);
},
```

The toArray() method on UIAElementArray converts the element array object, unique to UI Automation because of all the filtering and querying methods, to a normal JavaScript array. Once we have a simple JavaScript array we call map() on it, which calls the given function on each of the elements and returns a new array mapped to that function's results. Here, the end result is an array of strings—the names of the cell labels in the table view. We then pass that array to a new assertion function we will write to compare arrays.

Let's put this in our env.js file alongside our other assertion building blocks:

```
08-AppData/step01/automation/env.js
function assertEqualArrays(array1, array2, failMsg) {
    var failMsg = "Arrays not equal: " +
                        array1.toString() + " != " + array2.toString();
    assert(array1.length === array2.length, failMsg);
    for (var i = 0; i < array1.length; i++) {
        assert(array1[i] === array2[i], failMsg);
    }
}
```

This assertion function checks the array length and then loops over each element index and makes sure both arrays match, using the triple equal operator that we discussed back in *Quick and Simple Assertion Functions*, on page 46. Otherwise, the assertion fails and we get a nice error message.

That's it! Profile the app in Instruments with a UI Automation template, import the automation/test_sorting.js test file into the script editor, and run it to see the tests pass as shown in the following figure.

▼ Test search term sorting	Pass
Sorting search terms by recent	Default
target.frontMostApp().toolbar().segmentedControls()[0].buttons()[0].tap()	Debug
Sorting search terms by name	Default
target.frontMostApp().toolbar().segmentedControls()[0].buttons()[1].tap()	Debug
Test passed	Pass

Figure 54—The sort tests are passing.

Application data packages are a simple and effective way to ensure your app starts in a consistent state. Don't forget to switch to the normal scheme when you want to build and run the app on a device with live data. This scheme will *replace existing data on purpose*. Be careful.

This technique has limitations. It works only when an app is built and run from Xcode. This package isn't bundled with ad hoc builds or installable from the command line, and isn't reapplied if the app is relaunched from Spring-board. It's also not dynamic. We're installing a static snapshot of application state along with the app bundle. If we have more-complicated needs for data setup, then we must turn to a dynamic data factory in our code. Let's study that next.

8.2 Seeding Data Dynamically with a Factory

Now that we know the sorting behavior works correctly, we want to double-check the app's performance when sorting a large number of search terms. Changing the sort order triggers row animations to show the cells shuffling around, and it's possible that a large number of cells could gum up the works. The question is, how do we get a thousand search terms in our table view?

Yes, we could manually enter the terms ourselves and save an application data package. Instead we'll dynamically generate the data. This sets up possibilities for more complex scenarios that would be cumbersome to manage as a set of data packages.

We're going to build a data factory in our Objective-C code and tell it to populate the Core Data object graph following a set of scenario steps at launch time. This gives us expressive flexibility to specify on the fly what our data should look like.

Building a Data Factory

There are many different ways we could build a dynamic data factory. We could read from .plist files or request generated data from a web service, but we don't have to get that complex for this app. We're using Core Data, so we just need a class that knows how to reuse the code we're already using for production.

In this application, I've chosen to represent the Core Data stack and all its pieces as a single instance of NBMDocument. This keeps track of the managed-object context, the persistent store coordinator, and the path to the data file all in one place. It owns the responsibility for the mundane parts of managing and resetting Core Data. The factory we build will communicate with this document to do what it needs to do.

Here's a high-level overview of how NearbyMe normally sets up the Core Data stack:

08-AppData/step02/NearbyMe/NBMAppDelegate.m
```
- (BOOL)application:(UIApplication *)application
didFinishLaunchingWithOptions:(NSDictionary *)launchOptions
```

```
{
    // Initialize data structures
➤   self.document = [[NBMDocument alloc] init];

    // Finish normal setup for the user
➤   [self.document setupDefaultDataIfEmpty];

    // ...
```

The document creation happens in two phases. First, the Core Data stack is initialized when the document is initialized. Then we send setupDefaultDataIfEmpty to the document to set up the data as the user sees it on first launch. This checks to see if the data store is empty. If so, then the method builds the three default search terms that we've seen in the list all along. There's no technical reason for this default data. This is merely a design decision on my part. When users launch the app with no data, they're given a nice default set of search terms to start with.

Our test data factory will run in between the Core Data initialization and the default data-setup phases, like so:

08-AppData/step03/NearbyMe/NBMAppDelegate.m

```
// Initialize data structures
self.document = [[NBMDocument alloc] init];

➤  NBMTestDataFactory *factory = [[NBMTestDataFactory alloc]
➤                                 initWithDocument:self.document];
➤
➤  [factory generateAThousandSearchTerms];

    // Finish normal setup for the user
    [self.document setupDefaultDataIfEmpty];

    // ...
```

We're hard-coding the factory to generate our test data for us. In Section 8.3, *Choose Your Own Adventure with Environment Variables*, on page 135, we'll cover how to turn this off or choose different scenarios, but for now we're just proving out the idea.

Let's start writing this data-factory class, NBMTestDataFactory, in the Tests directory where we're putting all the test-related code files. The document has everything the factory needs, so it makes sense to accept a document object on initialization:

08-AppData/step03/NearbyMe/Tests/NBMTestDataFactory.m

```
@interface NBMTestDataFactory ()
@property (nonatomic, strong) NBMDocument *document;
@end

@implementation NBMTestDataFactory

- (id)initWithDocument:(NBMDocument *)document
{
    self = [super init];
    if (self) {
        _document = document;
    }
    return self;
}

// ...
```

Now, let's experiment and build out the hard-coded method that walks through a scenario of steps to generate 1,000 search terms:

08-AppData/step03/NearbyMe/Tests/NBMTestDataFactory.m

```
- (void)generateAThousandSearchTerms
{
    [self resetDocument];
    for (int count = 0; count < 1000; count++) {
        int length = arc4random_uniform(10) + 4;
        unichar buf[length];

        for (int idx = 0; idx < length; idx++) {
            buf[idx] = (unichar)('a' + arc4random_uniform(26));
        }

        NSString *term = [NSString stringWithCharacters:buf length:length];
        [self addSavedSearchTerm:term];
    }
    [self saveDocument];
}
```

We need some way to clear out anything that's already there, so we'll plan to write a resetDocument method on this class. Then we loop 1,000 times and generate random strings to pass to the addSavedSearchTerm method, which we'll write soon. When we're done with the loop, we'll save the document with the saveDocument method.

Now we're ready to write the three methods that represent steps our scenario needs to perform. Start with the method that resets the document to an empty state:

```
08-AppData/step03/NearbyMe/Tests/NBMTestDataFactory.m
- (void)resetDocument
{
    NSError *error = nil;
    if (![self.document deleteAndReset:&error]) {
        NSLog(@"%s: Could not reset database\n%@",
                __PRETTY_FUNCTION__, error);
        abort();
    }
}
```

We're calling the deleteAndReset method on our NBMDocument instance. That's a method I wrote that tears down the Core Data stack, removes the existing storage file if it's there, and builds a new one. For this test data factory there's no need for robust error handling. If something goes wrong, then it is catastrophic and the tests shouldn't continue. That's why it's sufficient to log the error along with the location in the file using the __PRETTY_FUNCTION__ compiler macro, and then abort. We want an error like this to fail quickly so we're not distracted from the problem by weird behavior down the line.

Next we need to write the method to add a search term:

```
08-AppData/step03/NearbyMe/Tests/NBMTestDataFactory.m
- (void)addSavedSearchTerm:(NSString *)term
{
    [NBMSavedSearch insertEntityContext:self.document.managedObjectContext
                            withText:term];
}
```

We're calling a custom method I wrote on the NBMSavedSearch managed object class. This is the same method used by the NBMSearchViewController to create search terms in the live application, and there's no reason we can't use it here. We're passing in the managed object context from the document and passing along the string name of the term we want to add.

Finally, we need a method to save the document:

```
08-AppData/step03/NearbyMe/Tests/NBMTestDataFactory.m
- (void)saveDocument
{
    NSError *error = nil;
    if (![self.document save:&error]) {
        NSLog(@"%s: Could not save database\n%@",
                __PRETTY_FUNCTION__, error);
        abort();
    }
}
```

Our document knows how to save itself, so we're reusing that and calling it here. And just like we did in the resetDocument method, we're handling the error by having the method fail quickly and loudly so we can fix it before continuing the tests.

The result is a completely self-contained factory object that knows how to talk to our Core Data stack and reuses the production code to manipulate the data. By writing common steps as separate methods on the class, we end up with scenario methods that are small and descriptive about what they produce.

Fixing the Sorting Performance Bug

With our data factory ready to do our bidding, let's check our sorting-animation performance. Build and run the app in Xcode. After launch, the data factory will kick in and replace any data that's already there with 1,000 random search terms. Tap on the sorting controls in the app; we see it pause for a moment with a white flash while everything is reordered. It's not unusable, but it's not good enough for us and it could be a hint of a deeper problem.

We could follow the techniques in Chapter 7, *Automating Performance Tests*, on page 101, to record and play back the steps to reproduce the problem while benchmarking the app to hunt down the cause. However, to stay focused on the task at hand, I'll leave that as an exercise for you. Here's a hint for where the problem lies.

All the reordering animation happens in the sortSwitchChanged method that is invoked when you tap on the segmented control to switch the sort order. Let's look at how it works:

08-AppData/step04/NearbyMe/NBMSearchViewController.m
```
- (IBAction)sortSwitchChanged:(UISegmentedControl *)sender
{
    NSArray *oldObjects = [self.fetchedResultsController fetchedObjects];

    [self refreshFetchedResultsController];
    [self.tableView beginUpdates];
    for (int i = 0; i < [oldObjects count]; i++) {
        NBMSavedSearch *search = [oldObjects objectAtIndex:i];
        NSIndexPath *oldIndexPath = [NSIndexPath indexPathForItem:i inSection:0];
        NSIndexPath *newIndexPath =
        [self.fetchedResultsController indexPathForObject:search];
        [self.tableView moveRowAtIndexPath:oldIndexPath
                               toIndexPath:newIndexPath];
    }
    [self.tableView endUpdates];
}
```

The method starts by asking the NSFetchedResultsController to give us back *all* the managed objects as an array in the old sort order. That right there should be a warning sign. It's asking Core Data to fetch all 1,000 terms just to sort the few visible ones.

The mundane work to refresh the fetched results controller happens in the refreshFetchedResultsController method. It prepares the controller with the new sort order based on which button is selected. Feel free to inspect that method on your own; it's not necessary for the problem at hand.

Once the results controller is up to date with the new sort order, we loop over *all* the original 1,000 objects and tell the table view that it needs to animate the cells for each object from the old to the new index paths.

This is a great example where the code is technically correct but solves the animation problem too simply and leaves us with a performance hit. The code is very straightforward to understand at a glance, but now that we want to handle a large number of search terms, we need to trade readability and add some complexity to this method to speed it up.

We only want to reorder the visible rows, moving some around, inserting ones that are now visible, and removing cells that are now offscreen. Overall, the method gets much more complex but speeds up tremendously:

08-AppData/step05/NearbyMe/NBMSearchViewController.m
```
- (IBAction)sortSwitchChanged:(UISegmentedControl *)sender
{
    NSArray *oldIndexPaths = [self.tableView indexPathsForVisibleRows];
    NSMutableArray *oldVisibleObjects = [NSMutableArray array];

    for (NSIndexPath *path in oldIndexPaths) {
        [oldVisibleObjects addObject:[self.fetchedResultsController
                objectAtIndexPath:path]];
    }

    [self refreshFetchedResultsController];

    [self.tableView beginUpdates];
    for (int i = 0; i < [oldVisibleObjects count]; i++) {
        NBMSavedSearch *search = [oldVisibleObjects objectAtIndex:i];
        NSIndexPath *oldIndexPath = [oldIndexPaths objectAtIndex:i];
        NSIndexPath *newIndexPath =
            [self.fetchedResultsController indexPathForObject:search];

        if ([oldIndexPaths containsObject:newIndexPath]) {
            [self.tableView moveRowAtIndexPath:oldIndexPath
                                   toIndexPath:newIndexPath];
        } else {
```

```
        [self.tableView deleteRowsAtIndexPaths:@[oldIndexPath]
                    withRowAnimation:UITableViewRowAnimationAutomatic];
        [self.tableView insertRowsAtIndexPaths:@[newIndexPath]
                    withRowAnimation:UITableViewRowAnimationAutomatic];
      }
    }
    [self.tableView endUpdates];
}
```

We have to keep track of the original array of visible index paths, loop over them to get the originally visible search terms, refresh, and loop again to decide how to animate the old to the new index paths with the standard table view animation commands. The key change is that we build a mutable array out of only the visible objects, not *all* the objects like we fetched before. Although this looks much more complicated and has an extra loop in it, it is much faster.

Now when we build and run the app, tapping the sort buttons animates instantaneously.

Checking Our Work

Technically, we've achieved our goal and solved the performance problem, but we shouldn't just stop there. We might have introduced a behavior bug with the drastic change we made. The good news is that we already wrote a sorting behavior test for our application in Section 8.1, *Seeding Data in Xcode with Application Data Packages*, on page 121. Let's use it to double-check our work.

First we'll build a scenario method on our data factory that sets up the terms the way our sorting test expects:

08-AppData/step06/NearbyMe/Tests/NBMTestDataFactory.m
```
- (void)generateSortingBehaviorTestTerms
{
    [self resetDocument];
    for (NSString *term in @[@"apple", @"orange", @"banana", @"kiwi"]) {
        [self addSavedSearchTerm:term];
    }
    [self saveDocument];
}
```

That was easy! We're reusing the methods on our data factory to express the scenario in a nice and concise domain language. We specify the terms in this order for the same reason we did so when we set up the data package: so they are sorted properly by descending creation time in the table view. To make this work we merely swap out the scenario method in our app delegate:

08-AppData/step06/NearbyMe/NBMAppDelegate.m
```
NBMTestDataFactory *factory = [[NBMTestDataFactory alloc]
                                initWithDocument:self.document];
```
➤ `[factory generateSortingBehaviorTestTerms];`

Now profile the app in Instruments with an Automation template, import the sorting-behavior test file, and run it. The factory will ensure our app starts in the state the test requires, and the test will verify that we didn't break the sorting behavior after we made such a huge change to the table view controller.

We can use data factories like this in all kinds of situations, not just UI-level tests. If you're doing lower-level integration testing and need to set up some sample data with an in-memory NBMDocument, use this factory for that, too. The data factory is an Objective-C class that is statically compiled, so it is built and checked by the compiler right along with the rest of the code. In applications that are complicated to set up, this technique lets you build your scenarios out of reusable pieces and will save you lots of time and headaches.

Manually swapping out scenario methods in the app delegate works fine while experimenting. Ideally, we want a way to dynamically choose which factory methods to call, and that's what we'll tackle next.

8.3 Choose Your Own Adventure with Environment Variables

We fixed a performance bug and verified behavior with our generated test data, but we don't want to have to manually change the Objective-C code when we want to choose a data scenario. Instead we'll choose which message to send to the data factory on the fly during application launch based on an environment-variable value.

Every Unix process, including iOS and OS X apps, has a set of variables made visible through that process's environment. We can assign any string value we want to these environment variables through Xcode schemes, as we'll see in a moment, and even from the command line, which we'll use in Chapter 10, *Command-Line Workflow*, on page 165.

Rather than hard-code the call to generate the thousands of search terms in our app delegate, we'll build a new Objective-C object that will respond to environment variables. This object will prevent any test-setup code from running unless it sees that we are in a test environment, and will act as a traffic cop and direct other test-related code, like our data factory, to respond appropriately. In the end, we'll have an Xcode scheme that can trigger any data-factory scenario we select.

Setting Environment Variables in an Xcode Scheme

In our Xcode scheme, let's set an environment variable that will be the flag to hint that we are running in a test environment. This will protect our data factory and other test-related code from running accidentally.

Edit the NearbyMeUITests scheme like we did in *Loading Application Data Packages with Xcode Schemes*, on page 124. Select the Run action in the sidebar and choose the Arguments tab in the right-hand pane. In the middle of the window, you'll see a place to add environment variables and their values. Add a variable UI_TESTS and set the value to yes like we see in the following figure.

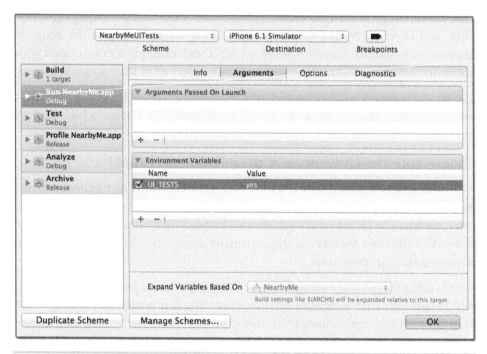

Figure 55—Setting an environment variable in an Xcode scheme

That's all there is to it. We'll use this first environment variable as the gate-keeper. It doesn't matter what the value is—we're going to check to see if it is set, and if it isn't, our test-setup object won't attempt to instruct the data factory to do anything.

The Profile action inherits these same environment variables from the scheme's Run action. This means we see identical results whether we run it directly or profile it in Instruments to use UI Automation. You can override the variables in the Profile action if you need to, but because this custom scheme is specifically for our UI tests, it's fine to leave them the same.

Reading the Environment from Objective-C

We need to read this environment variable in our application and respond to it. Rather than muddy up the app delegate object with a bunch of extra responsibilities and conditionals, we are better served building a separate object that knows what to do based on different variables.

Let's imagine what happens at the start of app launch. Where we were hard-coding a call to the data factory, we talk to our test-setup object instead, like so:

```
08-AppData/step07/NearbyMe/NBMAppDelegate.m
- (BOOL)application:(UIApplication *)application
didFinishLaunchingWithOptions:(NSDictionary *)launchOptions
{
    // Initialize data structures
    self.document = [[NBMDocument alloc] init];
➤   NBMTestSetup *setup = [[NBMTestSetup alloc] initWithDocument:self.document];
➤   [setup runIfInUITests];
    // ...
```

This looks pretty similar to how we were calling the data factory by hand. We instantiate a test-setup object with the dependencies it needs (just the NBM-Document in this case), and then we invoke runIfInUITests to have it do its magic. That method starts like this:

```
08-AppData/step07/NearbyMe/Tests/NBMTestSetup.m
- (void)runIfInUITests
{
    if (NBMEnvironment(@"UI_TESTS") == nil) return;
    // ...
```

Right at the top, we grab the value of the UI_TESTS environment variable and check to see if it is set. For our purposes, we don't care what the value is; we only need to check if it is there. If UI_TESTS isn't set, bail out of this method immediately, and the app will act normally.

To make it easy to grab environment-variable values, we'll write an NBMEnvironment() static C function like so:

```
08-AppData/step07/NearbyMe/Tests/NBMTestSetup.m
static inline NSString *NBMEnvironment(NSString *varName)
{
    NSDictionary *environment = [[NSProcessInfo processInfo] environment];
    return [environment objectForKey:varName];
}
```

The NSProcessInfo object gives us all kinds useful info about the running process wrapped in Objective-C idioms. By asking it for the environment, we get back an NSDictionary of the variables as key-value pairs. If a variable doesn't exist, we get back nil, which satisfies our check at the beginning of our runIfInUITests method.

Assuming the UI_TESTS variable is set in the environment, we can continue with our test setup:

08-AppData/step07/NearbyMe/Tests/NBMTestSetup.m
```
- (void)runIfInUITests
{
    if (NBMEnvironment(@"UI_TESTS") == nil) return;
    NSLog(@"UI_TESTS environment variable detected.");
    NSString *dataFactoryMessage = NBMEnvironment(@"DATA_FACTORY_MESSAGE");
    if (dataFactoryMessage) {
        [self sendMessageToDataFactory:dataFactoryMessage];
    }
}
```

When entering a test-specific mode such as this, log messages help us know what's going on. There's nothing more frustrating than chasing the wrong bug because we mistakenly used the wrong scheme.

Once we know we're in test-setup mode, we're ready to decide how to talk to the test components. We care only about the data factory right now, so we grab the value of the DATA_FACTORY_MESSAGE environment variable and check to see if it is set. If it is, we build a factory and use that variable's value as a method selector, like so:

08-AppData/step07/NearbyMe/Tests/NBMTestSetup.m
```
- (void)sendMessageToDataFactory:(NSString *)message
{
    NSLog(@"Sending message \"%@\" to data factory.", message);
    NBMTestDataFactory *factory =
            [[NBMTestDataFactory alloc] initWithDocument:self.document];
#pragma clang diagnostic push
#pragma clang diagnostic ignored "-Warc-performSelector-leaks"
    [factory performSelector:NSSelectorFromString(message)];
#pragma clang diagnostic pop
}
```

We print a note to the log that we're about to send a message to the data-factory object. Then we instantiate the factory with the document and send the message to the factory with performSelector. If we specify the wrong message, the app will crash immediately because of an unknown selector error, and we can check the log to see what happened.

We need the #pragma clang diagnostic marks to tell *Automatic Reference Counting (ARC)* that we know what we're doing when we compile. Otherwise ARC raises a warning about performSelector because it doesn't know whether it should retain the return value. What we're doing is perfectly safe since we're just sending the message and not doing anything with return values, so we'll suppress the warning until Apple works out the kinks with how performSelector behaves under ARC.

And, that's it! We're ready to try it out. Edit the NearbyMeUITests scheme and add the DATA_FACTORY_MESSAGE variable with the value generateAThousandSearchTerms. When you run or profile the app, the NBMTestSetup instance will see the UI_TESTS variable and send the message pulled from DATA_FACTORY_MESSAGE to the data factory. Our list of search terms will be replaced with the expected gibberish.

Using this technique, you can add a bunch of different environment variables to your scheme and check only the ones that matter to you in the moment, like in the following figure. Check out the 08-AppData/step08 directory in the book's example code to see it in action. You can even create separate schemes for the different scenarios you want to run. There's a lot of flexibility to mix and match values to create the custom environment you need for your tests.

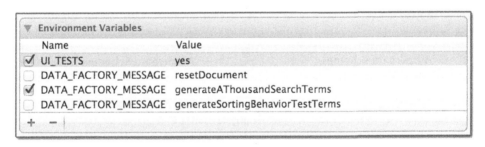

Figure 56—Checking different environment variables

We have a way to dynamically respond to the environment and set up the data how we want. But isn't it pretty risky to ship the app like this? Let's look into techniques to hide the test-setup code from release.

8.4 Hiding Test-Setup Code from Release

Since we're embedding a data factory into our application code, we should consider the impact this could have out in the wild. NearbyMe is a simple application, and an average user wouldn't be able to set environment variables to trigger these destructive data operations, so it doesn't matter much in this case. But if you have sensitive setup information for automated tests in your own applications, you may not want to compile the code paths that activate it, or even compile test-code files at all.

We're going to practice forking our code so test-specific setup code exists only in our test-specific build. We'll start by setting up a separate target that our test scheme will use. We'll utilize preprocessor conditional compilation to hide the lines that call test-setup code in the app delegate. Then we'll remove the test-specific code files entirely from the release-build target.

Setting Up a Separate Test Target

Xcode targets define how to build a specific product. Our project has only had one target, named NearbyMe, and the product it generates is an iOS app bundle. We want to fork our project and create two iOS app bundles that are almost identical. The only difference will be that our test-setup code exists in the test-specific bundle. The bundle we release to the App Store won't have it at all.

First, turn off the automatic creation of schemes in Xcode so it doesn't try to create a scheme for us when duplicating a target. Pull up the scheme editor by choosing Product > Scheme > Manage Schemes, and make sure the Autocreate Schemes check box is unchecked, as in the following figure.

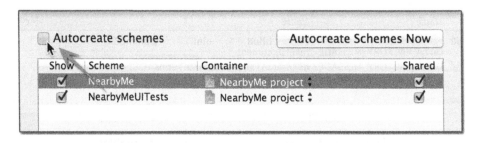

Figure 57—Uncheck the Autocreate Schemes check box.

Copy the existing target by selecting the project itself in Xcode's left-sidebar file browser. Then Control-click or right-click on the NearbyMe target and choose Duplicate, as in Figure 58, *Duplicate the target*, on page 141.

Let's clean up the build settings of our new target a bit and name everything appropriately. Rename the copy to NearbyMeUITests by double-clicking on the new target's name. Then, with the new target selected, click on the Build Settings tab in the main content area. Click the Basic and Combined lozenges under the tabs to simplify the view for editing. Then, change the Info Plist

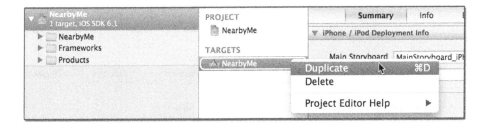

Figure 58—Duplicate the target.

name to NearbyMe/NearbyMe-Info.plist, and change Product Name to NearbyMe-UITests, as shown in the following figure.

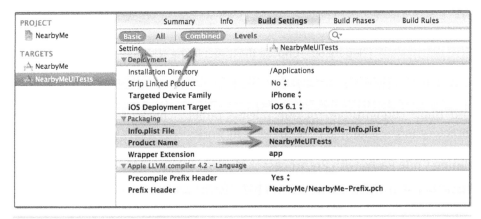

Figure 59—Cleaning up the target

Duplicating the target created a copy of the app's Info.plist file and named it NearbyMe copy-Info.plist. Find it in the left-sidebar file browser and remove it. For our purposes here, we want our test target to reuse as much as possible from the release target.

Almost done. We just need to tell our testing scheme to use this new testing target. Edit the NearbyMeUITests scheme, choose the Run action in the sidebar, chose the Info tab, and pick NearbyMeUITests.app from the drop-down list of executables, as in Figure 60, *Choose the target in the scheme*, on page 142.

Do the same thing for the Profile action. Unlike environment variables, the *Profile action does not inherit the executable setting* from the Run action. Since we want to use this target in UI Automation, we need to set it in the Profile action in the sidebar, as well.

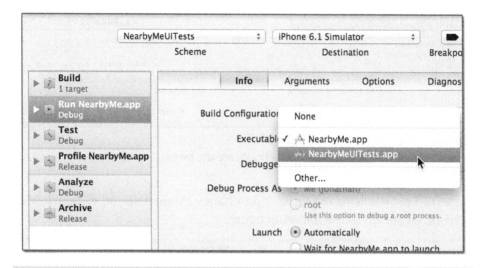

Figure 60—Choose the target in the scheme

We now have a completely separate test target that mirrors the same settings and build configuration of our release target. Check the 08-AppData/step09 directory in the example code to see it at work.

Hiding Code Paths with Preprocessor Macros

For a first step of protection, we can hide the lines where we create and execute our NBMTestSetup class in the app delegate using the C preprocessor. Before the Objective-C code even reaches the compiler, it passes through the preprocessor, which handles all sorts of housekeeping, like expanding #import statements and macro definitions into their final form.

We're not diving very deep into how the preprocessor works. For more info, check out *21st Century C [Kle12]*. But I do want to focus on the ability to include lines of code only in the presence of certain macros, like so:

```
08-AppData/step10/NearbyMe/NBMAppDelegate.m
- (BOOL)application:(UIApplication *)application
didFinishLaunchingWithOptions:(NSDictionary *)launchOptions
{
    // Initialize data structures
    self.document = [[NBMDocument alloc] init];
#ifdef COMPILE_UI_TESTS
    NBMTestSetup *setup = [[NBMTestSetup alloc] initWithDocument:self.document];
    [setup runIfInUITests];
#endif
    // ...
```

The preprocessor will allow the compiler to see the code within the #ifdef/#endif block only if the macro COMPILE_UI_TESTS is defined. Try this out by building and running the app to execute one of the data factories. Because we've not defined this macro yet, the NBMTestSetup class is never invoked. By hiding this line of code from production, it is impossible for anyone to control our test-setup code with environment variables.

We could just use the #define preprocessor directive somewhere in our header files to define this macro, but instead we're going to define the macro in the test target's build configuration so we don't have to alter our source files at all.

Click on the project in the left-hand sidebar to get back to the list of targets. Click on the NearbyMeUITests target and make sure the Build Settings tab is selected. Then click the All lozenge under the tab bar and type "preprocessor" into the search box so we find the Preprocessor Macros section (see the following figure).

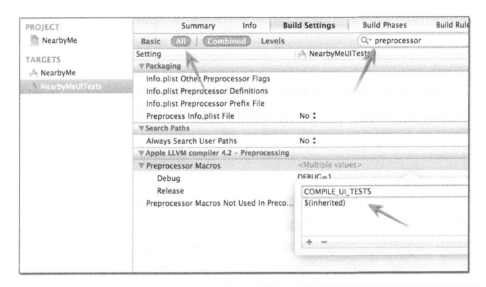

Figure 61—Adding custom preprocessor macros

Double-click on the line that says <Multiple values> to pop up the editor, and click the + button to override the settings for all the build configurations in this target. Type the string COMPILE_UI_TESTS and add another line with the string $(inherited). This second value tells the build system to inherit any preprocessor macros defined at a different configuration level, like the DEBUG=1 we see for the debug build configuration. We still want these things to bleed through.

Now when you build and run with the NearbyMeUITests scheme, it installs a separate NearbyMeUITests.app bundle that creates and invokes the NBMTestSetup object. When you build and run with the NearbyMe scheme, it installs the NearbyMe.app bundle with an app delegate that never even tries to run our test-setup code.

Removing Entire Files with Targets

Sometimes leaving out the setup lines isn't enough. If you are using special credentials for testing or talking to a secret part of an API, then you definitely don't want any code paths or resources in the app bundle for clever people to find and reverse-engineer.

The good news is that because we already have a separate test target, excluding whole files from release is easy. In the Xcode file browser, select the NBMTestSetup.m file, and in the right-sidebar inspector, make sure the first tab is selected so we're looking at the file settings. Then uncheck the box next to the NearbyMe target in the Target Membership section, as in the following figure.

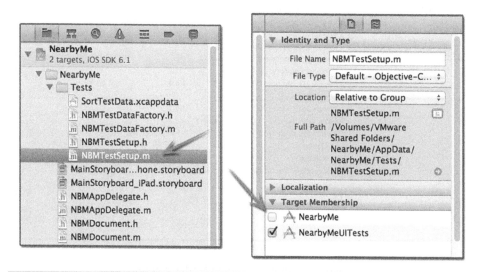

Figure 62—Excluding files from a target

That simple flick of the wrist is all you need to hide that entire class from the App Store. Do the same thing for the NBMTestDataFactory.m file for good measure. The next time we build and run the application with the main NearbyMe scheme, *none* of our test code is compiled at all. Check out the 08-AppData/step12 directory in the code accompanying the book for this example.

The Dangers of Complexity

Phew! That's a lot of work to keep test code out of the release. Is it worth it? You'll need to weigh the complexity costs to decide for your apps. Maintaining a second target like this can be a pain. You have to keep all the files straight and make sure you add new code files to both targets. If you ever get linker errors about missing class names, it's most likely because the target you're building for is missing a reference to a code file it expects. When working on the test-related code, you need to activate your test-specific scheme because syntax highlighting and autocompletion work only for files that are members of the active build target.

You also now have many more moving parts to worry about when juggling multiple build configurations and targets. The app compiled for release is quite different than the app compiled for testing. Every time we add conditional build steps like this, we introduce another layer of complexity where bugs that you wouldn't normally catch while developing can hatch.

Since NearbyMe doesn't have any secrets to hide, the code in the rest of the book isn't going to care about a separate testing target. The environment-variable checks are sufficient to guard against any user error. If a power user jailbreaks a device and wants to poke around NearbyMe, I think we can assume they're smart enough to back up their data.

We've practiced a few techniques to seed our application's state. We set up a separate testing scheme so that we can quickly build and run our app with a different environment. We have a way to communicate with the app at launch time through environment variables, and we explored options to hide potentially destructive test-setup code from the release build. Congratulations. This is nontrivial work. You've earned experience points in Xcode-build workflows.

Next we'll use some of the test-setup pieces we started here to tackle another headache of UI automation testing: stubbing external services.

CHAPTER 9

Stubbing External Services

Up to this point, we've been writing our tests with hope that the simulator always thinks it's in San Francisco and that OpenStreetMap data is consistent. As local businesses rise and fall, the search results displayed by NearbyMe will change, which means our behavior tests could fail even though the behavior is correct. Our tests are *fragile*–coupled to the state of external services we don't control. That's fine while learning, but now we're ready to address it.

We don't care if OpenStreetMap really finds the right results in downtown San Francisco. There's nothing we could do about it, anyway. And it's Apple's responsibility to assure that Core Location reads the right data from the GPS hardware. We don't want our tests to check the accuracy of these services; we want to test *our app's responses to these services*.

To isolate our app from the outside world we'll need to study a few techniques to stub external dependencies so they do our bidding. We'll talk a bit about how Xcode and UI Automation let us control the geographical location reported to our app. We'll build a fake version of OpenStreetMap that always returns the same JSON result when we ask it the right questions. And we'll even experiment with stubbing more complicated services within the application itself by building a facade we control in our test environment. By the end, we'll have a set of options at our disposal to reduce uncertainties for test suites of iOS applications.

9.1 Choosing a Geographical Location

Apps like NearbyMe depend on the user's location to do their work. Different locations mean we will get different results, so we need to figure out some way to get consistent, reliable coordinates back from Core Location.

Apple's already done the work for us and provides two simple hooks. One uses a special file format that Xcode loads when it runs the app. The other uses an interface exposed to UI Automation for setting the coordinates on the fly in our scripts. Let's explore both.

Choosing the Location in an Xcode Scheme

In Section 8.1, *Seeding Data in Xcode with Application Data Packages*, on page 121, we first used Xcode schemes to choose an application data package that completely replaced the sandbox with whatever we had captured previously. We can also use a scheme setting to choose a starting location that the simulator or device reports to the app. In fact, we've been using this all along.

The project code that comes with this book is already set to use downtown San Francisco, California, as the starting location. The simulator seems to use this location by default, but there's no guarantee that Apple will continue this convention, and it might change based on the user's locale. Choosing the location explicitly in an Xcode scheme gives our project some consistency as we work through the code examples in this book, and it ensures that building to test on a device will override the real GPS coordinates and use our chosen location instead.

There are already a bunch of cities across the world built in and ready to choose. Make sure the NearbyMeUITests scheme is selected in Xcode, pull up the scheme editor by choosing Product > Scheme > Edit Scheme, and choose any location you need from the Run action's pop-up menu, as in Figure 63, *Choosing a GPS location in Xcode*, on page 149.

But we don't have to settle for just these locations. All we have to do is add to the project a GPX file with contents like the following, which represents the location of my hometown of Akron, Ohio:

```
09-Stubbing/step01/NearbyMe/Tests/Akron, OH.gpx
<?xml version="1.0"?>
<gpx version="1.1" creator="Xcode">
    <wpt lat="41.0814" lon="-81.5192"><name>Akron, OH</name></wpt>
</gpx>
```

Copy this file into the Xcode project and choose this file name in the scheme editor's location pop-up menu. When you run or profile the app from Xcode, it will think you're in downtown Akron looking for something to do.

Like the application data packages, GPX files are snapshots that are given to the app when it launches, and they work only when the application is installed

Figure 63—Choosing a GPS location in Xcode

from the Xcode GUI. If we need real-time flexibility in our tests, we can turn to UI Automation's special API to exert more control.

Setting the Location on the Fly in UI Automation

We can use two methods on UIATarget to communicate with the Core Location services right from within our automation scripts. To see this at work, profile the app in Instruments from Xcode and, using a UI Automation template, enter the following in a fresh script:

```
09-Stubbing/step02/automation/sandbox.js
var target = UIATarget.localTarget();
target.setLocation({
    latitude: 41.0814,   // Akron, Ohio
    longitude: -81.5192
});
```

The setLocation() method takes a simple dictionary of latitude and longitude coordinates. If you want to specify more details, like altitude and speed, then you can use setLocationWithOptions() instead and pass in an additional dictionary. Core Location will reflect this new data immediately to the app.

It can be a pain to plug in raw coordinates when you need to choose cities, so I like to wrap this in a method that gives a higher-level meaning. Let's instead set the location based on city name, like this:

```
09-Stubbing/step03/automation/sandbox.js
#import "env.js";

App.setLocation("Akron");
```

We're importing the test environment we've built, and we'll add a method onto our App object that we started building in Chapter 6, *Strategies for Testing Universal Apps*, on page 79. We have very modest needs, so we can simply look up downtown locations by key in a JavaScript dictionary, like so:

```
09-Stubbing/step03/automation/lib/App.js
var App = {
    setLocation: function(name) {
        var locations = {
            "Akron":          { latitude: 41.0814, longitude: -81.5192 },
            "San Francisco": { latitude: 37.7873, longitude: -122.4082 }
        };
        var coords = locations[name];
        if (!coords) throw "Could not find coordinates named " + name;
        this.target().setLocation(coords);
    },
    // ...
};
```

Indexing into a coordinate dictionary by name and throwing in some error checking for good measure gives us a really simple way to dynamically make our app think it's running in different parts of the globe. There's no need to add travel money to the QA budget!

Note that if you use this UI Automation technique to choose a location while testing on an actual device, it will continue to think it's in that location even when the test is done and the app is closed. You need to soft-reset the device to return it to using the real GPS coordinates.

Stubbing location services is the easy part. It's all built in by Apple. Next we'll venture outside of the Xcode environment and wrangle an external network dependency that is simple enough for us to sufficiently fake.

9.2 Faking a Network-Service API

As it is right now, our app derives its usefulness from OpenStreetMap, a relatively simple black box. We hand it a rectangle of geographical coordinates and a search string, and it returns a JSON array of dictionaries that we parse. There's neither authentication nor any other hoops to jump through to get the information. That makes this an ideal candidate to practice building a fake service.

We're going to build a simple web server to return consistent JSON results given a box around a geographical point. We can make the data whatever we want, and it will never change unless we change it. We'll then learn how to point the app at our fake server when running in the test environment. Our tests will no longer depend on the current state of the OpenStreetMap API. For all our app knows, it will be talking to the real thing.

Building an HTTP Service

As judged by the numerous flame wars on Hacker News and Reddit, building a web service is a very personal thing. You can use whatever tool you want to accomplish this, but here I will use the Sinatra web framework built in the Ruby language because it has a very lightweight command interface.[1]

For your convenience, I've bundled everything we need to run our fake server right in the project step directories for this chapter. You don't need to go through the steps to install anything while you're learning about it here. Feel free to explore how to set it up on your own machine at your leisure.

Let's take a quick tour through this fake web service and find out the minimum we need to talk to the app:

09-Stubbing/step04/bin/fakeosm.rb
```
require File.dirname(__FILE__) + "/rubygems/local"
require "sinatra"
```

We start by setting up the Ruby package manager, RubyGems, so we can require the Sinatra web framework into our script file. The first line tells Ruby to use local copy of the gems bundled with our project. If you installed Sinatra on your system and want to try it out, you can replace that first line with just require "rubygems". Once RubyGems is primed and ready to go, we require the Sinatra framework and then we can get into the real meat of the web service:

09-Stubbing/step04/bin/fakeosm.rb
```
get("/search") do
  content_type(:json)
  query = params["q"]
  box   = extract_viewbox(params["viewbox"])

  # ...
end
```

Here we call a Sinatra function to declare a path handler. The do and end keywords denote a Ruby block, which you can think of like Objective-C blocks. In this case, we're declaring a handler that Sinatra will execute when it receives an HTTP GET request to the /search path.

---

1.   http://www.sinatrarb.com

The content_type() method is part of the Sinatra framework, and we're using it to declare the Content-Type HTTP header so the client knows this is JSON. Whatever string we return from this block will be the content body.

The params statement yields a Ruby dictionary that lets us access the URL query parameters we need, such as the search-term query and visible viewbox.

To use this viewbox, we need to do a bit of string-manipulation magic. The parameter comes in as a comma-separated string representing a box of geographical coordinates. Let's write a function that extracts from that string and returns an array of real numbers:

09-Stubbing/step04/bin/fakeosm.rb

```ruby
def extract_viewbox(viewbox_string="0,0,0,0")
  viewbox_string.split(",").map{|v| v.to_f}
end
```

We're just splitting the string on the commas and coercing the values to Float objects in a classic Ruby one-liner way. Returns are implicit in Ruby; the value of the last expression is automatically passed back. Now we have enough information to respond with the appropriate JSON:

09-Stubbing/step04/bin/fakeosm.rb

```ruby
get("/search") do
  content_type(:json)
  query = params["q"]
  box   = extract_viewbox(params["viewbox"])

➤   # Only know about coffee in downtown San Francisco
➤   if query == "coffee" && box_contains_point(box, 37.7873, -122.4082)
➤     File.read("san_fran.json")
➤   else
➤     "[]"
➤   end
end
```

We only need this to work in San Francisco, so we have a simple check that the query is "coffee" and that the center of downtown is located within the view box. Let's write the box_contains_point() method to do the bounds-checking:

09-Stubbing/step04/bin/fakeosm.rb

```ruby
def box_contains_point(box, lat, long)
  box[0] < long && box[1] > lat && box[2] > long && box[3] < lat
end
```

If the query and the point match, then we read the contents of san_fran.json in the root of the project directory and implicitly return it from the block. If they don't match, then we return a string that represents an empty JSON array. Sinatra takes whatever string comes out of the block as the response body.

The result is that we have a very simple endpoint with just enough smarts for our tests. Let's try it out before we plug it into the app. In the terminal, make sure you are in the project directory and run this command to start the server:

```
ruby bin/fakeosm.rb
```

Then, in another terminal window, run this command to make a network request with curl:

```
curl "localhost:4567/search?viewbox=-122.42,37.79,-122.39,37.77&amp;q=coffee"
```

A whole bunch of JSON dumps out to the screen. To make sure our simple logic is working, run that command again but change the q parameter to something other than coffee. Our server returns an empty JSON array.

You can make a fake service as smart or as simple as you need to get the work done. If we needed results for several locations, you could build some kind of mapping mechanism to load different data files near different coordinates. For our application, all we care about are the results in San Francisco. This is enough behavior to help us smoke out problems with our app trying to use the data from the OpenStreetMap API.

Pointing the App to the Fake Server in Test Mode

When we introduced the NBMTestSetup class, back in Chapter 8, *Setting Up Application Data*, on page 121, we called it at the start of the app delegate to make sure our application's data starts in the right state. If the UI_TESTS environment variable is set, like it is in our testing scheme, then our test-setup code will run. This is the perfect place to tell NearbyMe to talk to our fake API instead of OpenStreetMap:

```
09-Stubbing/step05/NearbyMe/Tests/NBMTestSetup.m
- (void)runIfInUITests
{
    if (NBMEnvironment(@"UI_TESTS") == nil) return;

    NSLog(@"UI_TESTS environment variable detected.");

    NSString *dataFactoryMessage = NBMEnvironment(@"DATA_FACTORY_MESSAGE");
    if (dataFactoryMessage) {
        [self sendMessageToDataFactory:dataFactoryMessage];
    }

➤   [OpenStreetMapService setHost:TestOSMServiceHost];
}
```

The `OpenStreetMapService` class is a lightweight abstraction built into NearbyMe to talk to the OpenStreetMap API. It takes a Map Kit rect and a query, crafts the appropriate URL, and calls back with the raw JSON results. Architecting the app to funnel all collaboration with an external service through a single point gives us the freedom to change it without disturbing the rest of the application.

The service is hard-coded to talk to the host at nominatim.openstreetmap.org. Since this must be set to something local in our test environment, we can use a static variable at the file scope and a class method, like so:

```
09-Stubbing/step05/NearbyMe/OpenStreetMapService.m
static NSString *OSMAPIHost = @"nominatim.openstreetmap.org";
@implementation OpenStreetMapService

+ (void)setHost:(NSString *)host
{
    OSMAPIHost = [host copy];
}

// ...
```

Declaring this variable outside the class definition makes it global in the sense that it is visible to every instance, but declaring it as static makes it local in that it is not accessible outside of the code in this file. The compiler will ensure that it starts with the real host string by default, and we can then change it on the fly using this setHost: class method.

So, what will this fake host be? If we are building and running this on the simulator, then we can make the host localhost:4567 since everything is running on the same machine. But what about running this on the device, as we'll certainly want to do? Let's use a preprocessor conditional, like we did in *Hiding Code Paths with Preprocessor Macros*, on page 142, to choose the host based on a flag Apple provides in the SDK:

```
09-Stubbing/step05/NearbyMe/Tests/NBMTestSetup.m
#if TARGET_IPHONE_SIMULATOR
#define TestOSMServiceHost @"localhost:4567"
#else
// Replace with your Mac's hostname
#define TestOSMServiceHost @"snarkbait.local:4567"
#endif
```

This TestOSMServiceHost expression is what we pass in to the setHost: method in our test setup. Obviously, you'll need to substitute your own Mac's hostname. But as long as the device is on the same local network as the Mac, it can identify it by hostname over Bonjour and talk to the fake server over port 4567.

Now to make sure our fake server is running and that the app thinks it's in San Francisco, we choose the location as we did in Section 9.1, *Choosing a Geographical Location*, on page 147. Launch the app, choose "coffee," and *boom*. Drag the map away from downtown and refresh. No results. We've faked a web service. We'll get the same results every time.

Let's tweak our iPhone test suite to match these results. First change test_suite.js to make sure we set the location to the city we are testing in:

09-Stubbing/step05/automation/test_suite.js
```
"use strict";

#import "env.js";

App.setLocation("San Francisco");

// ...
```

Now that we have a consistent geographical location and consistent behavior from our fake server, let's change the assertions that depend on points of interest:

09-Stubbing/step05/automation/test_suite.js
```
test("Searching for 'coffee' in downtown San Francisco", function() {
    SearchTermScreen.tapTerm("coffee");
    ResultsScreen.showList();
    ResultsListScreen.assertResult("Sightglass Coffee, 0.7 mi");
    ResultsScreen.goBack();
});

test("Searching for 'coffee' on the map in San Francisco", function() {
    SearchTermScreen.tapTerm("coffee");
    ResultsMapScreen.assertPinNamed("Sightglass Coffee");
    ResultsScreen.goBack();
});
```

Profile the app and load up a UI Automation template in Instruments with this suite file. Run it, and the success of our tests no longer depends on the state of OpenStreetMap. If a test fails, we know it's because of something we did.

Faking an external service works in some situations, but what if the dependency is an internal Apple framework or a service so complicated that it's more trouble to fake that it's worth? Next let's look into building facades in our app.

9.3 Wrapping Service APIs in a Facade

Imagine this scenario: an app needs to authenticate with Facebook using OAuth. We trigger a URL launching Mobile Safari so the user can log in. After authenticating, Facebook kicks the user back to the app with the token that gives us what we need. How would we test that?

Unfortunately, we can't. Apple doesn't expose any interprocess control to us through the automation interface. Once the app goes in the background, we're out of luck. Since Mobile Safari wasn't launched by Instruments, we can't talk to it from our tests.

In-app purchasing, Game Kit, and iCloud are other situations that are out of our control. We may want to test how our UI behaves if the user has purchased an item or not, but we don't want to spend time reverse-engineering the in-app purchasing protocol to figure out how to fake it.

We can address challenges like this by stepping back from the problem a bit. There isn't a one-size-fits-all solution, but some strategic thinking can help. Rather than trying to fake the services directly, we can hide them behind a facade that we write in our application code. Then, in the test environment, we stub out the facade and tell it how to behave.

In our project, faking the OpenStreetMap API is pretty straightforward. But for the sake of discussion, let's say we want to switch to use Map Kit's new MKLocalSearch mechanism, introduced in iOS 6.1, to find points of interest. We have no clue how Map Kit communicates with Apple's back end, and it would be a pain for us to stub externally. Instead, we'll study how NearbyMe hides these details behind a facade, decoupling our application from the needs of the service, so we can eventually stub it *internally*.

Separating Responsibilities

As it is right now, the results view controller of NearbyMe doesn't communicate with OpenStreetMap directly. It's not the view controller's job to know about HTTP issues or raw JSON responses. In our application's problem domain, our view controller knows about "points of interest." We're modeling that by having an NBMPointsOfInterestService object that fetches the raw JSON from the OpenStreetMapService and converts it into the model objects that our view controller expects, like so:

```
09-Stubbing/step05/NearbyMe/NBMPointsOfInterestService.m
- (void)findByText:(NSString *)query
         within:(MKMapRect)rect
{
```

```
OSMSCallback callback = ^(NSArray *results, NSError *error) {
    if (error) {
        [self.delegate poiService:self didFailWithError:error];
    } else {
        NSArray *pointsOfInterest =
                  [self pointsOfInterestFromAPIArray:results];
        [self.delegate poiService:self didFetchResults:pointsOfInterest];
    }
};

[OpenStreetMapService searchText:query within:rect completion:callback];
}
```

In our callback for the OpenStreetMapService, we check whether we get an error back. If so, we send it to the delegate, which is the view controller in this case. If not, then we run the JSON results through our local method pointsOfInterest-FromAPIArray: that builds an NSArray of NBMPointOfInterest objects from the response that we then pass on to the delegate.

In effect, we have separated the work to fetch data into three layers. At the bottom, we have a service object that knows how to talk to OpenStreetMap directly. At the next level, we have our facade service object that converts raw results from the searching service into application domain objects. And at the very top we have the view controller that consumes these domain objects and feeds the UI.

Switching to Map Kit

Because the app is structured to fetch points of interest through the facade service object, we easily convert to using Map Kit's search by altering the findByText:within: method on NBMPointsOfInterestService like so:

```
09-Stubbing/step06/NearbyMe/NBMPointsOfInterestService.m
- (void)findByText:(NSString *)query
            within:(MKMapRect)rect
{
    MKLocalSearchRequest *request = [[MKLocalSearchRequest alloc] init];
    request.naturalLanguageQuery = query;
    request.region = MKCoordinateRegionForMapRect(rect);

    self.search = [[MKLocalSearch alloc] initWithRequest:request];

    [self.search startWithCompletionHandler:completion];
}
```

We create an MKLocalSearchRequest object and give it the cues it needs to find results. We retain a reference to it while it does its work, and then we execute with this completion handler:

09-Stubbing/step06/NearbyMe/NBMPointsOfInterestService.m

```
__weak NBMPointsOfInterestService *weakSelf = self;
MKLocalSearchCompletionHandler completion =
    ^(MKLocalSearchResponse *response, NSError *error) {
        if (error) {
            [weakSelf.delegate poiService:self didFailWithError:error];
        } else {
            NSArray *pois = [weakSelf pointsOfInterestFromResponse:response];
            [weakSelf.delegate poiService:self didFetchResults:pois];
        }
    };
```

We need the obligatory weak reference to self to make we sure we don't cause a retain cycle in the completion handler. In the block, we either report an error or convert the response to an array of NBMPointOfInterest objects to pass back to the delegate. Converting the response is just a straightforward loop over the array we got back from Map Kit, which we're doing in this separate method:

09-Stubbing/step06/NearbyMe/NBMPointsOfInterestService.m

```
- (NSArray *)pointsOfInterestFromResponse:(MKLocalSearchResponse *)response
{
    NSMutableArray *pointsOfInterest = [NSMutableArray new];

    for (MKMapItem *item in response.mapItems) {
        NBMPointOfInterest *poi = [[NBMPointOfInterest alloc] init];
        poi.title = item.name;
        poi.coordinate = item.placemark.location.coordinate;
        [pointsOfInterest addObject:poi];
    }

    return pointsOfInterest;
}
```

For every MKMapItem returned from the Map Kit local search, we create an NBMPointOfInterest object that our app knows how to consume and manipulate. This is the same process used to handle the results from OpenStreetMap, except this time we're looping over MKMapItem objects instead of a JSON array.

Facades like this are a powerful way for our applications to decouple from external services we can't control. If OpenStreetMap went away for some reason, we just follow these steps to swap in a different provider. This kind of decoupling makes it easier to forge results for our tests. We don't need to know any of the details of the MKLocalSearch mechanism. We merely have to stub this facade in our test environment. Let's do that next.

9.4 Stubbing a Facade with Data in the App Bundle

Now that we've seen a service-facade architecture at work in the application, controlling it in our test environment is quite straightforward. We'll override the findByText:within: method in a subclass NBMPointsOfInterestService and have it return whatever data we want. We need to figure out how to use this special subclass instead of the normal one when running in the test environment.

Using a Subclass Instead of a Superclass

There are a lot of ways to substitute one class for another on the fly. We could conjure elaborate Objective-C runtime magic by changing pointers or swizzling, but we don't have to get that fancy here. We have full control over these classes, and all we have to do is follow this rule: always create an instance of NBMPointsOfInterestService using the +service class-factory method. Class-factory methods are often used as convenience constructors for autoreleased objects, but they also comes in handy when we need to do our own ad hoc version of a class cluster.[2]

In our class-factory method, we construct an instance out of a class we choose on the fly:

```
09-Stubbing/step07/NearbyMe/NBMPointsOfInterestService.m
static Class pointsOfInterestServiceClass = nil;
@implementation NBMPointsOfInterestService

+ (instancetype)service
{
    return [[pointsOfInterestServiceClass alloc] init];
}
// ...
```

Instead of saying [[self alloc] init], we are initializing whatever class is in the static file-scoped variable pointsOfInterestServiceClass. How do we populate this on app launch? We can't have the compiler set an initial value in this variable because class objects are currently not compile-time constants. Instead, we use the standard +initialize class method:

```
09-Stubbing/step07/NearbyMe/NBMPointsOfInterestService.m
+ (void)initialize
{
    if (self != [NBMPointsOfInterestService class]) return;
    pointsOfInterestServiceClass = self;
}
```

---

2. http://developer.apple.com/library/ios/documentation/general/conceptual/CocoaEncyclopedia/ClassClusters/ClassClusters.html

The Objective-C runtime guarantees that this initialization method will be called before any other method is called. It's possible for the method to be called more than once if a subclass doesn't also override +initialize, so we need to check the class to make sure we run this code for only this specific class.[3]

This lets us initialize the value of our static file-scoped pointsOfInterestServiceClass variable with self. During normal operation, the +service class-factory method will behave as it always had and our app will get real results from Map Kit.

We need a way for our test environment to set this static variable. Let's build a class method that will act as a setter:

09-Stubbing/step07/NearbyMe/NBMPointsOfInterestService.m

```
+ (void)setServiceClass:(Class)newClass
{
    pointsOfInterestServiceClass = newClass;
}
```

Calling this changes the +service class-factory method's behavior and returns an instance of the substituted class instead.

We're going through this rigmarole because we don't want this service class to make decisions about the test environment on its own. We went to the trouble to create the NBMTestSetup object in Chapter 8, *Setting Up Application Data*, on page 121, because we want to isolate the decisions about test setup in one place. All our service class knows is that it could be swapped out. *By whom* and *to what* are the jobs of our test-setup code, and that's what we'll tackle next.

Loading Results from a .plist File in the Bundle

Now we're ready to build a stubbed subclass. It can be substituted anywhere the normal superclass would fit, but we'll have full control over it in our test environment. Let's change our NBMTestSetup class to stub this facade instead of stubbing OpenStreetMap like we did back in *Pointing the App to the Fake Server in Test Mode*, on page 153:

09-Stubbing/step07/NearbyMe/Tests/NBMTestSetup.m

```
- (void)runIfInUITests
{
    if (NBMEnvironment(@"UI_TESTS") == nil) return;

    NSLog(@"UI_TESTS environment variable detected.");

    NSString *dataFactoryMessage = NBMEnvironment(@"DATA_FACTORY_MESSAGE");
```

---

3. http://www.mikeash.com/pyblog/friday-qa-2009-05-22-objective-c-class-loading-and-initialization.html

```
   if (dataFactoryMessage) {
       [self sendMessageToDataFactory:dataFactoryMessage];
   }
```

➤   `[NBMPointsOfInterestServiceStub stubServiceSuperclass];`

```
}
```

Now create an NBMPointsOfInterestServiceStub subclass with the +stubServiceSuperclass method on it that will do the substitution:

09-Stubbing/step07/NearbyMe/Tests/NBMPointsOfInterestServiceStub.m

```
@implementation NBMPointsOfInterestServiceStub

+ (void)stubServiceSuperclass
{
    [NBMPointsOfInterestService setServiceClass:self];
}

// ...
```

This method does the dirty work and tells the real points-of-interest service class to instantiate this stub instead. Now for the fun part. Override the find-ByText:within: method in our subclass to return canned results:

09-Stubbing/step07/NearbyMe/Tests/NBMPointsOfInterestServiceStub.m

```
- (void)findByText:(NSString *)query
            within:(MKMapRect)rect
{
    NSArray *pois = @[];

    MKMapPoint downtownSF = MKMapPointForCoordinate(
                                CLLocationCoordinate2DMake(37.7873, -122.4082));

    if ([query isEqualToString:@"coffee"] &&
            MKMapRectContainsPoint(rect, downtownSF)) {
```

➤   `pois = [self pointsOfInterestFromRawResultsInBundleNamed:@"san_fran"];`

```
    }

    [self.delegate poiService:self didFetchResults:pois];
}
```

Just like we did back in *Building an HTTP Service*, on page 151, we're going to hard-code results for "coffee" near downtown San Francisco. As long as the map box encloses the coordinates of downtown, we'll return an array of results. Otherwise, we'll return an empty array.

Let's experiment and first build the method that returns our model objects:

09-Stubbing/step07/NearbyMe/Tests/NBMPointsOfInterestServiceStub.m

```
- (NSArray *)pointsOfInterestFromRawResultsInBundleNamed:(NSString *)name
{
➤    NSArray *results = [self rawResultsFromBundleFileName:name];
    NSMutableArray *pointsOfInterest = [NSMutableArray new];
    for (NSDictionary *result in results) {
        NBMPointOfInterest *poi = [[NBMPointOfInterest alloc] init];
        poi.title = result[@"title"];
        poi.coordinate = CLLocationCoordinate2DMake(
                        [result[@"lat"] floatValue],
                        [result[@"lon"] floatValue]);
        [pointsOfInterest addObject:poi];
    }
    return pointsOfInterest;
}
```

We're building a new array of NBMPointOfInterest objects based on the data we're reading from a file.

So, where do these results come from? To give this stub more power, I want to load them from a file that will live in the app bundle itself. If we're running the app in the simulator, we could access any path on the host Mac and read files from the project directory. But if we want to use this stub on a device, the results have to come from the app sandbox. Bundling it as a resource in the app is a fine way to do it.

To keep this as simple as possible, we'll encode our canned results in Apple's .plist file format, an XML format that describes serialized collections and dictionaries in Cocoa:

09-Stubbing/step07/NearbyMe/Tests/san_fran.plist

```
<plist version="1.0">
<array>
        <dict>
                <key>lat</key>
                <string>37.7799405</string>
                <key>lon</key>
                <string>-122.4076637</string>
                <key>title</key>
                <string>Rancho Parnassus Coffee</string>
        </dict>
  <!-- ... -->
```

I generated this by using writeToFile:atomically: on an NSArray instance I built up from real results, but you can just as easily construct your own using Xcode's built-in .plist editor. Make sure the file is part of your Xcode project and is included in the target like we discussed in *Removing Entire Files with Targets*, on page 144.

Now let's find the file in the bundle and load its contents:

09-Stubbing/step07/NearbyMe/Tests/NBMPointsOfInterestServiceStub.m
```
- (NSArray *)rawResultsFromBundleFileName:(NSString *)name
{
    NSURL *fileURL = [[NSBundle mainBundle] URLForResource:name
                                              withExtension:@"plist"];
    NSArray *results = [NSArray arrayWithContentsOfURL:fileURL];
    if (!results) {
        NSLog(@"Error parsing JSON from %@\n%s",
              fileURL, __PRETTY_FUNCTION__);
        abort();
    }
    return results;
}
```

We look up a .plist file with the given name in the bundle, load it into an NSArray, and do some very simple error checking. If the load failed, we want to abort immediately with a reason why so that we aren't confused by missing data down the line.

And that's it! We've successfully stubbed our points-of-interest service. When the app runs with the UI_TESTS environment variable set, our NBMTestSetup class will instruct our stub to substitute itself for the real service. The results view controller thinks it is talking to a service that talks to Map Kit, but in reality we're just loading the results from a .plist file in the bundle.

I've included a .plist file in the project included with the book that is an exact duplicate of the JSON results we returned from our fake OpenStreetMap server earlier. This means our test suite will still "just work." Load it up in UI Automation and run it. There's nothing else to be done!

Stubbing services with a facade layer in the app takes some forethought and modification. It's a bit more work to maintain than stubbing a service with an external fake like we did earlier, but it gives us flexibility to work with complex dependencies.

We've scratched the surface with a few techniques to rein in external services and make our test scripts more reliable. Testing of any kind requires trade-offs. Do we stub internally or externally? Do we load data from a file or do we generate it on the fly? These decisions require creativity and planning. I hope the themes here spark your imagination as you tackle your own app dependencies.

These last two chapters have given us a lot of food for thought, from setting up the application in a repeatable state to decoupling our tests from external influences. Next we're going to learn how to completely isolate our tests and run scripts automatically from the command line.

CHAPTER 10

Command-Line Workflow

The Xcode IDE and Instruments GUI integrate well together and provide a quick feedback loop while iterating on UI Automation test code. But we still have a lot of manual steps involved. We must fire up an Automation template, import script files, run them, and check the results before importing the next one. This is fine during development, but we need something more automatic that can run all our scripts at once with a single command.

This is a great reason to explore a command-line workflow with UI Automation. Using shell scripts we'll write ourselves, we'll execute the automation scripts we've been writing throughout this book, one after the other. Ideally, we want a script that will build and run NearbyMe for both the iPad and iPhone simulators, executing the appropriate test files for both device families. We can call this script from anywhere, maybe with an SCM hook after code is pushed up, or on a regular nightly interval by a continuous-integration machine. Knowing your way around the command line opens up a lot of opportunities to save time so you can focus on other things.

Let's start by practicing with the raw commands that build the app bundle and run our automation scripts. Then we'll use the Rake build tool that comes with OS X to help us wrap the complex commands in something more manageable. Along the way, we'll learn how to reset the simulator and fully isolate our test runs, and even run our tests on an attached device. By the end you'll have a low-level understanding of the process and pitfalls, and you'll have ideas that you can apply to your own applications.

10.1 Practicing with the Raw Commands

For our first adventure, we need to understand the raw commands and what they do. Alas, Apple's command-line dev tools often feel like a hostile environment. They change things all the time, and we need to write our shell scripts defensively. We're going to look at the build process to create an app bundle in a known location, and then look at the automation process that launches Instruments, pointing it at the app bundle and the script we want to run.

To prepare, make sure the command-line tools are installed and ready on your machine. Pull up the Xcode preferences, switch to the Downloads tab, and click the Install button for the command-line tools if they're not already installed; see the following figure.

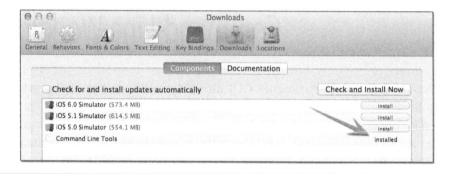

Figure 64—Ensure command-line tools are installed.

Run the clang command from a terminal window. If you see the following error message, then you're good to go:

```
clang: error: no input files
```

Building the App Bundle in the Right Place

Building within the Xcode IDE is as simple as pressing ⌘-B, but we need a way to automate the build without involving the GUI so we can guarantee that we have a fresh copy of the app bundle every time we run our tests.

The xcodebuild command gives us what we need. Let's see it in action with our NearbyMe project. Pull up a terminal window and change to the 10-Command-Line/step01 directory that is part of the book's sample code. Type in this command exactly as shown, including the backslashes and line breaks:

10-CommandLine/step01/run_tests.sh
```
xcodebuild \
  -project NearbyMe.xcodeproj \
  -scheme NearbyMeUITests \
  -configuration Release \
  -sdk iphonesimulator \
  CONFIGURATION_BUILD_DIR=/tmp/NearbyMe \
  TARGETED_DEVICE_FAMILY=1 \
  build
```

When you press ↵ after the last line, a flurry of activity scrolls past your eyes as Xcode does its work to build the application. Since this command is so long, we're breaking it into multiple lines with the backslashes that let the shell know this is all one command. The lines are easier to read this way and will be easier to edit when we incorporate this into a build script.

Some of these parameters are optional as xcodebuild tries to infer defaults where it can. But to help you learn and to avoid ambiguity, we'll explicitly state parameters we need for NearbyMe. Let's break this command down piece by piece.

- -project NearbyMe.xcodeproj—This selects the project file. Often Xcode can just figure it out, but it doesn't hurt to specify it. If you have a workspace, you'll need to use the -workspace parameter instead.

- -scheme NearbyMeUITests—This chooses the test-specific scheme we built in Chapter 8, *Setting Up Application Data*, on page 121. That way, any conditionally compiled code that sets up our test environment will be there waiting for us.

- -configuration Release—This tells the compiler which build configuration to use. Since Xcode's Profile action builds the app for the Release configuration when launching in Instruments, we'll do the same thing here for consistency.

- -sdk iphonesimulator—For this demonstration we're compiling for the x86 architecture to link against the simulator version of the SDK. We'll revisit this because we need to dynamically change this parameter to iphoneos if we want to build an app bundle for the device instead.

- CONFIGURATION_BUILD_DIR=/tmp/NearbyMe—This is an Xcode configuration setting that says to put all the build results in a specific directory. Depending on how you or your team have Xcode set up, the final app bundle could land anywhere. To keep things consistent, I like to explicitly override the destination here in this command. Xcode will create this directory if it's not already there.

- TARGETED_DEVICE_FAMILY=1—This tells Xcode what device family to target. For a universal app like NearbyMe this setting is normally 1,2, and we're overriding it so that Xcode sets the appropriate key in the app bundle's Info.plist to force it to be treated as an iPhone-only app.

We need to do this because Instruments always launches universal apps in the iPad simulator, which won't work if we want to run our iPhone behavior tests. Until we have more control over how Instruments launches, we need to trick it into thinking this is just for iPhone. You can ignore this parameter if your app supports only one device family.

- build—This string instructs Xcode to do a build for this project. We'll also need to run this command with clean, which tells Xcode to remove all the build products out of the configuration build directory. Cleaning and building help us ensure that no funky build artifacts are left over to mess with our test results.

Where do settings like CONFIGURATION_BUILD_DIR and TARGETED_DEVICE_FAMILY come from? You can find these and more by viewing the project or target settings in the Xcode IDE and choosing Editor > Show Setting Names to expose something like the following figure.

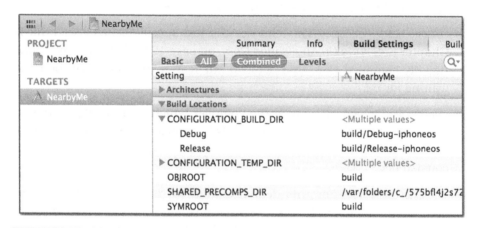

Figure 65—Viewing the setting names

All of those settings are overrideable from the command line. This is great if you have some special needs for your automated test builds but don't want to spin up yet another build configuration or scheme to satisfy those needs.

That's the essence of how to build NearbyMe from the command line. When we wrap this in a build script we'll make the parameters more dynamic, but for now we just want this command to work so we can run our iPhone automation-test suite next.

Running an Automation-Test Script

We have the NearbyMe app bundle built with our test scheme and stored in a known location. We're almost ready to tell Instruments to load that bundle into the simulator and run one of our test scripts, but there are two details to address before the instruments command can work.

When run from the command line, Instruments needs a directory where it dumps trace recordings. So, in the project directory, run mkdir automation_results. If you're revisiting this section and the directory already exists, remove it and start over with an empty one, just to have a common starting point.

Instruments also needs a trace-document template that it will use to run the UI Automation script. Launch Instruments manually by switching to the Xcode IDE and choosing Xcode > Open Developer Tool > Instruments through the Xcode menu. Pick the standard Automation template and then choose File > Save as Template and save it in the automation directory of the NearbyMe project. Name it Template, and it will receive the .tracetemplate extension.

Close the Instruments and iOS Simulator applications before continuing. Sometimes you'll encounter weird race conditions among Apple's tools that have GUI front ends. It's simpler to just close them when running from the command line.

With our app bundle built and our automation template in the right place, we're ready to roll. Type this command into the terminal, backslashes and all, and press ↵:

```
10-CommandLine/step01/run_tests.sh
instruments \
  -t automation/Template.tracetemplate \
  -D automation_results/Trace \
  /tmp/NearbyMe/NearbyMe.app \
  -e UIARESULTSPATH automation_results \
  -e UIASCRIPT automation/test_suite.js \
  -e UI_TESTS 1 \
  -e DATA_FACTORY_MESSAGE resetDocument
```

Two things may happen to you that you'll have to correct. You will likely get an authentication prompt asking you to grant Instruments permission to inspect this application. Type in your administrator password to continue. This prompt comes up from time to time as a security measure because Instruments has deep interprocess power. We'll discuss how to completely disable this later if need be.

It's also possible that the test will fail if this is the first time this app bundle has been installed in the simulator. Our test suite doesn't know how to handle the location-permissions alert yet, and iOS won't grant permission to use GPS coordinates unless we confirm it. If this happens to you, just launch the

Settings app and grant the app permission in the Privacy settings before trying to run the command again.

Once the command runs, another flurry of console activity scrolls past your eyes in the terminal, and you'll see output similar to the trace log we're familiar with in the Instruments GUI.

Let's break down the command and study it:

- -t automation/Template.tracetemplate—This says to use the custom template with the Automation instrument we just created.

- -D automation_results/Trace—This tells instruments where to put the trace document that will be generated from this template. This is the same document you'd get if you save the trace-recording results from the GUI interface. Double-clicking this file will open it in Instruments, and you can peruse past runs and all the data collected.

- /tmp/NearbyMe/NearbyMe.app—This is the app-bundle path we built earlier. If your test scheme generates a different bundle name, like we experimented with in Section 8.4, *Hiding Test-Setup Code from Release*, on page 139, then you'll want to reference that here instead.

- -e UIARESULTSPATH automation_results—All the -e parameters set environment variables that will be visible to the application and UI Automation. This one tells UI Automation where to write an XML copy of the automation trace log. This is the same content written to the trace document, but UI Automation also writes them out as XML files, which makes it easier to postprocess the results if you need to.

- -e UIASCRIPT automation/test_suite.js—The UIASCRIPT variable holds the path to the JavaScript automation file itself.

- -e UI_TESTS 1—The last two environment variables should look familiar. This one tells the test-setup code we wrote back in Chapter 8, *Setting Up Application Data*, on page 121, that we're in UI-testing mode. We used to set these environment variables in the Xcode schemes when building with the IDE; now we're setting them here for our command-line workflow.

- -e DATA_FACTORY_MESSAGE resetDocument—Our data factory reads this environment variable and will dutifully reset the app document to its default state for this test run.

Yes, every parameter of this monstrously long command is required. This is just begging for us to wrap it in a script and alter the necessary parameters on the fly. We'll get to that in a bit.

Cleaning Up Debug Messages and Instruments Authentication

By default, UI Automation prints a lot of debug messages during test runs. I like that because it helps me understand the steps UI Automation takes. If it's more than you need, consider these two simple commands to disable them:

```
defaults write com.apple.dt.InstrumentsCLI UIAVerboseLogging -int 4096
defaults write com.apple.dt.Instruments UIAVerboseLogging -int 4096
```

These alter the user defaults for both the Instruments command-line utility and the GUI, turning off the UI Automation verbose logging. If you want to turn them back on, just run these commands:

```
defaults delete com.apple.dt.InstrumentsCLI UIAVerboseLogging
defaults delete com.apple.dt.Instruments UIAVerboseLogging
```

Note that although you can run xcodebuild from any user account you want, you can only run the instruments command from an account that is logged in to the desktop. The simulator needs the window manager to be fully initialized, and that requires a logged-in user.

When we first ran the instruments command, you may have been prompted to grant it permission to control another process. This is a security feature because Instruments takes full control even if initiated by a limited user account, and you don't want to let a rogue process get ahold of it.

Still, this protection gets in the way and defeats the purpose of a script that runs without our intervention. If you have a dedicated machine whose sole responsibility is to pull down the code and run it regularly, then you'll want to disable this security feature.

Through a bit of research and my own testing in an OS X virtual machine, I've isolated a change to a configuration file in OS X Mountain Lion that controls the privileges of applications that ask for the ability to hook into other processes.

WARNING! Running this command *will make your machine less secure.* Apple has this protection in place for a reason, and OS X is built assuming it is there. Use this only on a specially built machine that is well isolated. Also, there's no guarantee that this will work (or even be necessary) in future versions of OS X.

Now that I've sufficiently scared you, here's the command that does the dirty work:

```
# WARNING: This purposefully weakens security
sudo /usr/libexec/PlistBuddy \
    -c "Set rights:system.privilege.taskport:allow-root true" \
    /etc/authorization
```

This uses the PlistBuddy command to set a key in the /etc/authorization file that will grant Instruments permission to control other processes whenever it wants. You may still be prompted the very first time you run it, but after that the authorization will be on autopilot.

Phew! That's a lot effort to understand what running two commands does to build and automate our tests. The raw building blocks are important, but we need to take more control of the process.

Let's look into managing these commands a little better with a robust build environment that can run our automation scripts one after the other for both the iPhone and iPad simulators.

10.2 Automating the Build-and-Run Process with Rake

There are many ways to script things in Unix land. Here I will use Rake, the build tool written in Ruby and inspired by the make command. I think Ruby's heritage as a shell-scripting language makes it a fine choice to build tasks out of smaller methods with annotation about what they do. Everything we're going to use in Rake works out of the box on OS X, with no dependencies to install. Of course, if you feel strongly about a different scripting platform, feel free to translate these tactics to your tool of choice.

We'll build two Rake tasks. The first is a simple one that cleans out old trace results. The second is the main task that does the full execution of our test suite on both device types. We'll build it out of reusable Ruby methods that do the dirty work to tell the xcodebuild and instruments commands to work their magic.

Cleaning Old Trace Results

Let's start by building a simple task to wipe out the automation_results directory. As Instruments fills this directory, it sometimes gets confused when the directory grows large over thousands of runs. If you ever get the message "instruments error: (null)," when trying to run your tests, it means that something was corrupted in the automation traces. Cleaning out this directory is a good practice, and this is a great task to prime our Rake script.

Start a file named Rakefile in the project's root with these contents:

```
10-CommandLine/step02/Rakefile
BUILD_DIR              = "/tmp/NearbyMe"
APP_BUNDLE             = "#{BUILD_DIR}/NearbyMe.app"
AUTOMATION_TEMPLATE    = "automation/Template.tracetemplate"
RESULTS_PATH           = "automation_results"
OUTPUT_TRACE_DOCUMENT  = "#{RESULTS_PATH}/Trace"

# If the automation_results directory isn't there, Instruments balks.
mkdir_p RESULTS_PATH
```

Things like build path, template, and bundle name need to be shared among our tasks, and it's nice to make them configurable. We're putting them in Ruby constants at the top of the file, where we can easily see them and adjust them as our project's needs change. Any identifier that starts with a capital letter is a constant, but it's customary to spell out value constants like these in all caps.

Notice the #{...} syntax when constructing the value of APP_BUNDLE. We're using one of Ruby's interpolation techniques to build strings out of pieces. In this case we want to build the app-bundle path using the already defined BUILD_DIR constant. Since shell scripting is ten percent inspiration and ninety percent string manipulation, we'll be using techniques like this a lot.

Right after defining the constants, we call Rake's convenient mkdir_p() method, which runs a mkdir -p shell command to ensure the RESULTS_PATH directory exists. Instruments throws an unintelligible fit if this directory is missing, so we'll make sure that never happens by running this command every time Rake is invoked. Parentheses are optional in Ruby, and they are commonly left off for statements like this that aren't part of a larger expression.

Next let's declare the Rake task to clean the results directory:

```
10-CommandLine/step02/Rakefile
desc "Remove the automation_results directory and start fresh"
task "clean_results" do
  rm_rf RESULTS_PATH
end
```

The desc() Ruby method annotates the following task defined with the task() method. Our task, "clean_results," will execute the Ruby block that tells Rake to run the rm -rf shell command to remove the automation-results path. Like the mkdir_p() method we saw earlier, Rake comes with several of these shell methods for common commands.

And that's it for our first task! All we have to do is type rake clean_results↵ in the terminal, and the automation_results directory will be removed, to be re-created on the next run of Rake.

Building and Running in the "Default" Task

Now let's write the Rake task that will execute xcodebuild and instruments for us. We'll compose it out of reusable methods that will build the app bundle and run the automation scripts appropriate for both the iPhone and iPad simulators:

```
10-CommandLine/step02/Rakefile
desc "Run appropriate tests for iPhone and iPad Simulators"
task "default" do
  clean

  build "iphone"
  automate "automation/test_suite.js"

  build "ipad"
  automate "automation/test_suite_ipad.js"

  close_sim

  puts "\nWin condition acquired!"
end
```

We're naming this task "default" because that's the task name that Rake runs when we type rake↵ all by itself at the command line. This Rakefile is all about automating our automation tests, after all. Inside, we call a series of methods that let us describe the process involved to run our test scripts. We want to clean the build products to start fresh, build for the iPhone device family, run our iPhone automation tests, and do the same for the iPad. Each of these methods will hide the nasty long commands behind a simple and easy-to-read interface. A glance at this task tells us exactly what will happen to run our tests.

Notice at the end of the task we print a string to standard out with a happy message to let us know it succeeded. We'll reach this message only if nothing went wrong. Any shell command that fails and returns a nonzero status code will cause Rake to abort immediately with a nonzero status code, which is exactly what we want if any step in this process fails.

Let's flesh this task out by building each of the supporting methods.

Controlling xcodebuild

We have to tell the xcodebuild command to do different things depending on whether we are cleaning or building, and whether we are targeting the iPhone or iPad simulator. We can solve this by splitting the responsibility to run the command into two layers.

At the highest layer, we have descriptive methods like clean() and build() that will delegate to the lower layer like so:

10-CommandLine/step02/Rakefile
```
def clean
  run_xcodebuild "clean"
end
```

To clean out the build products and start completely fresh, we need to pass the clean argument to the xcodebuild command, along with the project, scheme, and configuration build directory so it knows what to clean. Because of all these shared boilerplate parameters, we're wrapping the call to xcodebuild in a lower layer with our run_xcodebuild() method, like so:

10-CommandLine/step02/Rakefile
```
def run_xcodebuild extra_args
  sh %{
    xcodebuild \\
      -project NearbyMe.xcodeproj \\
      -scheme NearbyMeUITests \\
      -configuration Release \\
      CONFIGURATION_BUILD_DIR="#{BUILD_DIR}" \\
      #{extra_args}
  }
end
```

The sh() method is Rake's way of helping us run raw shell commands from within Ruby. It runs whatever string we give it and echoes the full command to standard out so we see all the variables expanded. I like to use the %{...} Ruby string-delimiter syntax when I give multiline shell commands to sh(), because it looks more like a code block and we don't have to worry about escaping double or single quotes that need to be in the command.

Notice the double instead of the single backslashes we used before to break the raw command lines for readability. Single backslashes would function fine here, but Ruby would then remove the line breaks before passing the string to the sh() method. I like to escape the backslashes so the shell sees them, too, because it makes the commands look cleaner when echoed. Reading the Rake output to find out how the variables and constants are interpolated can help debug problems. Remember: shell scripting is ninety percent string manipulation!

We're inserting the BUILD_DIR constant as the value of the CONFIGURATION_BUILD_DIR setting and using the string argument passed to run_xcodebuild() as the rest of the command line. Our clean() method calls this and passes in clean, so the net effect is that Xcode knows exactly where everything is when it needs to clean out any existing build products.

Note that we're wrapping the BUILD_DIR path in double quotes. Command-line tools treat spaces as argument separators and if we don't quote paths, then they will be misinterpreted as multiple arguments. It's wise to always wrap paths with quotes in shell scripts because we never know when we'll encounter a space, and it's notoriously difficult to debug.

With this lower-layer method doing the raw work to construct the xcodebuild command, we can use it in our build() method like so:

```
10-CommandLine/step02/Rakefile
def build type
  case type
  when "iphone"
    sdk = "iphonesimulator"
    fam = "1"
  when "ipad"
    sdk = "iphonesimulator"
    fam = "2"
  else
    raise "Unknown build type: #{type}"
  end

  run_xcodebuild "build -sdk #{sdk} TARGETED_DEVICE_FAMILY=#{fam}"
end
```

As we discussed earlier, we need to dynamically change the build parameters depending on the device family we're targeting in the simulator. We set the sdk and fam variables based on the type argument passed in to the method, and use them to finish constructing the argument string for run_xcodebuild().

Scripting Instruments and the Exit Status Code

The next method in our "default" task is automate(), which takes a script filename and builds the massively long parameter list for the instruments command:

```
10-CommandLine/step02/Rakefile
def automate script
  sh %{
    bin/unix_instruments \\
      -t "#{AUTOMATION_TEMPLATE}" \\
```

```
      -D "#{OUTPUT_TRACE_DOCUMENT}" \\
      "#{APP_BUNDLE}" \\
      -e UIARESULTSPATH "#{RESULTS_PATH}" \\
      -e UI_TESTS 1 \\
      -e UIASCRIPT "#{script}"
  }
end
```

Just like how we talked to the xcodebuild command before, we're using the sh()
method to build a command string by interpolating all the necessary values.
However, the sharp reader will notice that we're not calling the instruments
command directly. Instead, we're calling a wrapper script in our project,
bin/unix_instruments.

Remember that we want Rake to abort immediately if any of the commands
we run fail with a nonzero exit status code. The instruments command returns
a zero exit status code to indicate success even if a UI Automation test reports
a failure. This is because Instruments itself *successfully recorded its trace
with the Automation instrument.*

To solve this, I've written a wrapper script, included in the project, that is a
drop-in replacement for the command.[1] The script eavesdrops on the output
of instruments and remembers if it sees an error or JavaScript exception logged
in the output. If so, it exits with a nonzero status code; otherwise, it passes
along the status code that came out of the instruments command.

Feel free to read through it. There's some deep and dark shell-piping magic
going on that's irrelevant to our discussion here, so we'll just use this script
for what it is: an isolated black box that we can drop in when we need it, and
remove should Apple change the behavior of Instruments to report nonzero
status codes when UI Automation logs a failure.

Closing the Simulator

We've done the bulk of the work for this "default" Rake task, but we have one
final housekeeping method to write. Assuming the task succeeds and makes
it all the way through, we want it to close the simulator with the close_sim()
method:

10-CommandLine/step02/Rakefile
```
def close_sim
  sh %{killall "iPhone Simulator" || true}
end
```

---

1.   https://gist.github.com/jonathanpenn/1402258

There isn't an official way to control the simulator from the command line, so we're left to our own devices. Using the killall command is more effective than using something like AppleScript and doesn't leave the Simulator running in a weird state.

We need the strange || true tacked on at the end of the command to protect Rake because the killall command will abort with a nonzero status code if the process isn't running. We don't consider that a failure for our Rake script because we call this as an optional cleanup method. Appending the "|| true" tells the shell that if killall fails, it should execute the true command, which always succeeds.

And that's it! We have a single Rake task that will build and run some of our automated-behavior test scripts for both the iPad and iPhone simulators. Type rake↵ into the terminal; Xcode will build and Instruments will run with the familiar flurry of activity in the console. A much easier way to run our automated tests!

This is great for a start, but now let's enhance this powerful script to set environment variables on the fly for our test-setup needs.

10.3 Reading Environment Variables from Script Files

We have our basic behavior test suites running on both device families in the simulator, but what if we want to run tests that require more-complicated setup? For instance, our sorting test expects a different set of search terms than the default. We already went through the trouble of building our data factory to generate these in Chapter 8, *Setting Up Application Data*, on page 121, but we need a way to trigger methods on the factory with environment variables on the fly.

Let's dig into the problem by building a new Rake task that lets us focus on running just one test from the command line. That way we can run this test over and over while we tweak things to get them to work:

10-CommandLine/step03/Rakefile
```
desc "Focused test run. Things in progress."
task "focus" do
  clean
  build 'iphone'
  automate "automation/test_sorting.js"

  close_sim
  puts "\nWin condition acquired!"
end
```

We're reusing the same pieces from our "default" task, but this time we're only running our sorting-test script for the iPhone simulator. If we type rake focus↵, the script fails with this error among the output:

```
Script threw an uncaught JavaScript error: Arrays not equal:
coffee,sandwich,fish != kiwi,banana,orange,apple on line 30 of env.js
```

And this is why we need a way to tie our scripts to their expected application state. The test_sorting.js script should tell the app to generate these expected search terms, and our other script files should tell the app to use the default data.

There are many ways to pull this off, but here's a technique that can be useful and self-documenting. It lets us specify any number of environment variables to pass to the app and annotates the test script with the expected starting state. Put this comment at the top of automation/test_sorting.js:

10-CommandLine/step04/automation/test_sorting.js
```javascript
// DATA_FACTORY_MESSAGE=generateSortingBehaviorTestTerms
"use strict";

#import "env.js";

test("Test search term sorting", function() {
    // ...
```

We're establishing a convention that any JavaScript comment with the pattern KEY_ON_THE_LEFT=VALUE_ON_THE_RIGHT will be extracted and transformed into environment-variable parameters for Instruments.

To use this, let's alter our automate() method in the Rakefile so it extracts the special comments:

10-CommandLine/step04/Rakefile
```ruby
def automate script
  env_vars = extract_environment_variables(script)

  sh %{
    bin/unix_instruments \\
      -t "#{AUTOMATION_TEMPLATE}" \\
      -D "#{OUTPUT_TRACE_DOCUMENT}" \\
      "#{APP_BUNDLE}" \\
      -e UIARESULTSPATH "#{RESULTS_PATH}" \\
      -e UI_TESTS 1 \\
      -e UIASCRIPT "#{script}" \\
      #{env_vars}
  }
end
```

Before we call the bin/unix_instruments wrapper script, we extract the variables from the script with a utility method that returns them as a valid parameter string. We then tack that string onto the end of the command we pass to the sh() method.

Let's write the extract_environment_variables() method like so:

10-CommandLine/step04/Rakefile
```ruby
def extract_environment_variables script

  lines = File.readlines script
  arguments = []

  lines.each do |line|
    line.match(%r{^// (.+)=(.+)$})

    if $1
      arguments << "-e " + $1 + " " + $2
    end
  end

  arguments.join(' ')
end
```

There's a little bit of Ruby sleight of hand that I'm going to gloss over because it's not directly related to our goals, but we're basically looping over all the lines, and if any of them match a regular expression that looks like our pattern, we capture the left and right side of the equals sign and build a string with the properly formatted -e flags.

That's all we need to get this sorting test to work. Run rake focus↵, and it passes with fanfare!

We need to fix our other behavior tests to declare their environment variables, too, or else they will break if they see the sorting-test data:

10-CommandLine/step04/automation/test_suite.js
```javascript
// DATA_FACTORY_MESSAGE=resetDocument
"use strict";
// ...
```

10-CommandLine/step04/automation/test_suite_ipad.js
```javascript
// DATA_FACTORY_MESSAGE=resetDocument
"use strict";
// ...
```

And now that we're sure our tests files have the right state when they run, let's add this sorting test to our "default" task:

10-CommandLine/step04/Rakefile
```
desc "Run appropriate tests for iPhone and iPad Simulators"
task "default" do
  clean

  build "iphone"
  automate "automation/test_suite.js"
➤ automate "automation/test_sorting.js"

  build "ipad"
  automate "automation/test_suite_ipad.js"

  close_sim

  puts "\nWin condition acquired!"
end
```

Run rake↵ from the terminal, and all three automation-test files will run—two for the iPhone simulator, and one for the iPad. Our script files now have hints for how the application should set itself up on each run!

10.4 Resetting the Simulator to Test Permissions

We're moving faster now that we've tucked away the complexity of the raw shell commands in our Rakefile. Let's keep going and use our "focus" task to help us construct a new behavior test that asserts what users should see if they deny access to the GPS coordinates.

Users are asked for permissions only the first time the application launches after install. If we were testing this from the Instruments GUI, then we'd have to reset the simulator or remove the application between each run. Because we're building a shell script to automatically run our tests, we leverage that to reset the simulator automatically between each run.

First let's change our "focus" task to run a new test file we're going to write:

10-CommandLine/step05/Rakefile
```
desc "Focused test run. Things in progress."
task "focus" do
  clean

  build 'iphone'
➤ automate "automation/test_location_permission.js"

  close_sim

  puts "\nWin condition acquired!"
end
```

Now write this test script that asserts users see an alert if they don't approve the app for location services:

```
10-CommandLine/step05/automation/test_location_permission.js
// DATA_FACTORY_MESSAGE=resetDocument
"use strict";

#import "env.js";

test("User told to enable location services", function() {
    SearchTermScreen.tapTerm("coffee");
    var title = ""NearbyMe" Would Like to Use Your Current Location";
    AlertScreen.assertWithTitle(title);
    AlertScreen.cancel();
    delay(1);  // Wait for previous alert to vanish
    AlertScreen.assertWithTitle("Location Disabled");
});
```

We start at the top with the specially formatted comment telling our data factory to initialize with default data. We import our test environment, and then we construct our test. After tapping the "coffee" search term, we assert that we see the system alert asking for location permissions. We cancel that alert and wait a second for the alert to vanish before we check for the next alert that tells users that they disabled the location services and the app isn't very useful.

We must manually pause before checking for the new alert, because in the moments after we tap Cancel and the permissions alert is starting to vanish, our second assertion might think that the old alert is the one it should assert for. There's no way around it. We have to manually pause for this assertion.

We can't run this yet because we're not resetting the simulator. Normally you do this while the simulator is running through a menu command, and we could use AppleScript to automate it, but to keep things simple we're just going to completely erase the simulator data directory, which will be re-created the next time the simulator launches.

Let's do this in our automate() method in the Rakefile so that every time we try to execute a script, the simulator will be reset:

```
10-CommandLine/step05/Rakefile
def automate script
➤   reset_sim

    env_vars = extract_environment_variables(script)

    sh %{
      bin/unix_instruments \\
```

```
        -t "#{AUTOMATION_TEMPLATE}" \\
        -D "#{OUTPUT_TRACE_DOCUMENT}" \\
        "#{APP_BUNDLE}" \\
        -e UIARESULTSPATH "#{RESULTS_PATH}" \\
        -e UI_TESTS 1 \\
        -e UIASCRIPT "#{script}" \\
        #{env_vars}
    }
end
```

And then let's write the reset_sim() method to do the dirty work:

```
10-CommandLine/step05/Rakefile
def reset_sim
  close_sim
  sim_root = "~/Library/Application Support/iPhone Simulator"
  rm_rf File.expand_path(sim_root)
end
```

We're running our close_sim() method that we wrote earlier to close the simulator if it's running, because we're going to be removing data from underneath it. We expand the path to the simulator data root so that the tilde character (~) is substituted with the user's home folder, and then we remove it.

When we run rake focus↵, the simulator is completely reset, iOS asks the user for location permissions, we deny it, and then we check for the appropriate alert by title in response. Huzzah!

We have a slight problem to correct, though. Now that we're resetting the simulator for *every* automation run, we need to fix other relevant tests so they confirm the location-permissions alert. We didn't write our other behavior tests under this kind of environment, so we didn't have a reason to worry about it, but we do now.

For the tests we've written thus far, only our iPhone behavior tests in automation/test_suite.js access the map. We just need to ensure that we confirm the location-permissions alert when we first request the user's location:

```
10-CommandLine/step06/automation/test_suite.js
test("Searching for 'coffee' in downtown San Francisco", function() {
    SearchTermScreen.tapTerm("coffee");
➤   AlertScreen.confirmLocationPermission();
    ResultsScreen.showList();
    ResultsListScreen.assertResult("Sightglass Coffee, 0.7 mi");
    ResultsScreen.goBack();
});
```

Let's add this new method to the AlertScreen object so that it confirms the permissions alert if it shows up, like so:

10-CommandLine/step06/automation/lib/screens/AlertScreen.js

```
var AlertScreen = {
    // ...
    confirmLocationPermission: function() {
        this.target().pushTimeout(1);
        var alert = this.alert();
        this.target().popTimeout();
        if (alert.isValid()) {
            var title = alert.name();
            if (title.match(/Would Like to Use Your Current Location/)) {
                alert.defaultButton().tap();
            }
        }
    },
    // ...
};
```

This method gracefully degrades if the alert doesn't pop up, which means our tests will still work if we pull them up in the Instruments GUI and run them against an app that already has the permissions approved. We push a short timeout, long enough to give time for the alert to show, then we ask for an alert element and check to see if the result is valid and if the title matches the location-permissions alert. If so, we confirm it. If an alert never shows up, we move on.

Now our iPhone behavior-test file will be prepared if it sees the location-permissions alert. Before we run all our tests in the "default" task, let's add this new location-permission test to the set of iPhone tests:

10-CommandLine/step06/Rakefile

```
desc "Run appropriate tests for iPhone and iPad Simulators"
task "default" do
  clean

  build "iphone"
  automate "automation/test_suite.js"
  automate "automation/test_sorting.js"
➤ automate "automation/test_location_permission.js"

  build "ipad"
  automate "automation/test_suite_ipad.js"

  close_sim

  puts "\nWin condition acquired!"
end
```

Run rake↵, and all of our behavior tests run back-to-back and with complete environment isolation. A major win!

This is something we hinted at back in Chapter 8, *Setting Up Application Data*, on page 121, when we tried to set up the application state in as reliable a way as possible. There was only so much we could control from within our automation scripts and from within the app. Now that we are constructing a build system with full shell power at our fingertips, we can manipulate anything we want. By isolating our shell commands in appropriately named Ruby methods, we can adjust how they work if the process changes or Apple moves files around again.

We're almost done with our deep dive into command-line techniques. Let's finally turn our attention to running tests on attached devices.

10.5 Running Tests on an Attached Device

Running tests on the simulator is a great first line of defense for testing behavior, but it is important to check them on the device as well. There's just enough difference between the SDKs and architectures to make it worth our while to explore how to do it from the command line.

Instruments is quite capable of pulling this off, but we'll need to adjust how we build the application with xcodebuild. We also need to choose a different set of scripts depending on what device is connected. And we'll look into an unofficial hack that sometimes works to install the app automatically on a device marked for development. At least we'll wrap the mechanism in a part of the script that we can swap out with an official mechanism whenever Apple implements it.

Building for the Device

We first need to build a specific, test-dedicated Rake task that we can run on devices. Let's imagine how it could work:

```
10-CommandLine/step07/Rakefile
desc "Run appropriate tests for the connected device"
task "device" do
  $is_testing_on_device = true
  clean
  build "device"
  if connected_device_is_ipad?
    automate "automation/test_suite_ipad.js"
  else
    automate "automation/test_suite.js"
    automate "automation/test_sorting.js"
  end

  puts "\nWin condition acquired!"
end
```

This reuses the same methods as our "default" Rake task, but takes some detours in how we build and choose the tests to run. We first set a global Ruby variable as a flag that we are about to run a test on a device. Our automate() method will use this variable so that it knows it needs to pass the connected device UUID to the instruments command. More on that in a moment.

We need to tell xcodebuild that we're linking against the device SDK, so we're calling our build() method with the device string, which we'll handle like so:

10-CommandLine/step07/Rakefile

```
def build type
  case type
  when "iphone"
    sdk = "iphonesimulator"
    fam = "1"
  when "ipad"
    sdk = "iphonesimulator"
    fam = "2"
➤ when "device"
➤   sdk = "iphoneos"
➤   fam = "1,2"
  else
    raise "Unknown build type: #{type}"
  end

  run_xcodebuild "build -sdk #{sdk} TARGETED_DEVICE_FAMILY=#{fam}"
end
```

If this method sees that the type variable is device, we set the sdk variable to iphoneos and fam to 1,2. That way Xcode will build the app for the device SDK and ensure that the final bundle targets both device families. As mentioned before, if your application is only for iPhone or only for iPad, you can change the value here to whatever is appropriate for your project.

We have a bundle built for the device, but how do we know if we should run the iPad or iPhone tests? By using a bit of string-scraping trickery we can inspect the output of the ioreg command when it finds all devices that say they support iOS:

10-CommandLine/step07/Rakefile

```
def ioreg_output
  `ioreg -w 0 -rc IOUSBDevice -k SupportsIPhoneOS`
end

def connected_device_is_ipad?
  !ioreg_output.match(/"USB Product Name" = "iPad"/).nil?
end
```

The first method uses the backtick operator to run the ioreg command searching for iOS devices and return the output. The second method builds on top of this and does a regular-expression search to identify whether the first device found is an iPad.

Obviously, this is a fragile mechanism. Apple could change its identification scheme or the ioreg output format could evolve. Isolating that possibility here gives us only one place to worry about updating.

We know what tests to run, but now our automate() method needs to know the device ID to pass along to Instruments:

10-CommandLine/step07/Rakefile
```
def automate script
  reset_sim

  if $is_testing_on_device
    device_arg = "-w #{connected_device_id}"
  end

  env_vars = extract_environment_variables(script)

  sh %{
    bin/unix_instruments \\
      #{device_arg} \\
      -t "#{AUTOMATION_TEMPLATE}" \\
      -D "#{OUTPUT_TRACE_DOCUMENT}" \\
      "#{APP_BUNDLE}" \\
      -e UIARESULTSPATH "#{RESULTS_PATH}" \\
      -e UI_TESTS 1 \\
      -e UIASCRIPT "#{script}" \\
      #{env_vars}
  }
end
```

Here's where the $is_testing_on_device global variable comes in. We're not going to assume that we always want to test on a device if it is plugged in, which is why we're setting this flag in our device-specific tasks. We grab the connected device UUID and prepend the -w flag so we can pass it into the bin/unix_instruments command below it. If we don't set the global variable, then the device_arg variable will just be blank when interpolated into the shell command, and Instruments will try to run on the simulator as it has all along.

We grab the first connected device's UUID from the ioreg output like so:

10-CommandLine/step07/Rakefile
```
def connected_device_id
  ioreg_output.match(/"USB Serial Number" = "([A-z\d]+)"/) && $1
end
```

We're using regular expressions to find the serial number of the first connected iOS device. If you want to have this run on more connected devices in sequence, you can take steps to make this more robust.

Unfortunately, this command doesn't automatically install the app bundle on the device like it does on the simulator; at least, Apple hasn't chosen to do that at the time of this writing. We still need to specify a valid app bundle because Instruments uses the identifier information in the Info.plist file to know which app to run. However, the app must already be installed on the device.

So, let's satisfy that constraint by building and running the app for the NearbyMeUITests scheme in the Xcode IDE on your attached device. Once it launches, stop the app in Xcode and run rake device↵ from the terminal. Boom. Tests are running on the device. Even the test-setup code is properly executed.

You'll note that we left out the test for the location-permissions alert. We don't yet have a way to fully reset permissions for an application installed on a device. If Apple adds that capability in the future, it wouldn't be hard to include that test here, but this is a great illustration of the trade-offs of testing on the simulator vs. the device. We have more control over the simulator, but the device is what the app actually ships on. Insert well-reasoned and context-bound judgment here.

What About Automatically Installing on a Device?

This task works great as long as we build and install the app with the right scheme from the Xcode IDE. But is there a way to install automatically? If so, then we could set up a Mac as a faithful build server that pulls down the code and runs the tests against whatever device stays connected to it. Alas, there's no official way to do this yet, but there is an undocumented hack that works most of the time and can lead you in the right direction if this is critical for your workflow.

Fruitstrap is a small shell executable originally written by Greg Hughes that hooks into undocumented mechanisms to install bundles on devices marked for development.[2] Greg Hughes has since abandoned the project and encourages using one of the forks on GitHub, but at least we have the source to peruse. It still works most of the time as of Xcode 4.6.

If you'd like to see this in action, check out the 10-CommandLine/step08 directory in the sample code that comes with this book. I've put the fruitstrap binary in the bin directory, and I call it from the "device" task.

---

2.   https://github.com/ghughes/fruitstrap

I've seen fruitstrap get confused if Xcode or iTunes is running while you try to use it. Sometimes I have to reset my device. It's the only option we have at the moment while we wait for Apple to add this functionality, though.[3] Consider this an exercise for the reader. It's possible that fruitstrap will break in the near future from benign changes Apple makes to its infrastructure.

Yes, working with Apple's dev tools from the command line feels very hostile. The best strategy, as with any external dependency that we can't control, is to script and isolate those parts so they can be adjusted with a minimum of fuss.

And that wraps up the code-heavy portions of this book. You've walked through automation-testing an existing iOS application—from experimenting in Instruments to building a test suite to handling universal application idioms to performance testing, and capped off with a command-line workflow. Well done!

Next we'll look at some third-party testing tools and how they can help us write the best applications for our users.

---

3. You did file a duplicate bug report with Apple, right? http://bugreport.apple.com

CHAPTER 11

Third-Party Tools and Beyond

We've traveled a long and productive road learning how to work with UI Automation, from the basic elements to building our own tools for reuse. I believe starting with what comes out of the box in Apple's SDK gives you an advantage. There is less to install and learn up front while grasping the nuances, and you don't grow dependent on the "magic" behind the scenes in third-party libraries.

Now that we've reached a good understanding of the way UI Automation works, we'll look at the wider community's contributions. Whether you want to augment your UI Automation testing workflow or approach testing with an entirely different paradigm, we'll discuss where to go next.

This isn't an exhaustive list, but it reflects my own use and evaluation. I hope you walk away with a good perspective of the trade-offs and how to judge third-party resources for your own projects.

11.1 Enhancing UI Automation

The developer community around UI Automation is small but growing. Here are a few tools that you can learn from and that fit well within this book's scope.

Writing Tests with Tuneup JS

Tuneup JS is one of the original test frameworks for UI Automation, developed by Alex Vollmer.[1] I mentioned it back in *Choosing the Tools that Work*, on page 58, when we started to organize our test-script code. It comes with robust assertions like this test that checks the state of the whole screen:

---

1.   http://www.tuneupjs.org

```
test("Check the whole window", function(target, app) {
  assertWindow({
    navigationBar: {
      leftButton: { name: "Back" },
      rightButton: { name: "Done" }
    },
    tableViews: [
      {
        cells: [
          { name: "Fred Flintstone" }
        ]
      }
    ]
  });
});
```

Tuneup JS follows a common JavaScript testing paradigm, and it's straightforward to add your own assertions. You can drop it into the test suite we've been writing with a minimum of fuss. You only need to put #import "*path_to*/tuneup.js" at the top of your test-environment file and use Tuneup JS's functions instead of the ones we wrote.

It's also easy to read for a JavaScript beginner. If you'd like to see more real-world examples of testing in JavaScript and you're new to the language, this is a great place to start.

Finding Elements with Mechanic

If you come from the web-development world and have any experience with jQuery, you're probably going to love mechanic.js.[2] Jason Kozemczak built a query engine for finding arbitrary elements on the screen based on "element selectors" that resemble CSS selectors used with web pages. For example, we can tap a button with the name MyButton anywhere on the screen, like so:

```
$("button#MyButton").tap();
```

This is much simpler than traversing the element tree manually, but suffers from the same trade-offs we discovered when we wrote a recursive predicate search in Section 6.4, *Searching the Element Tree with Predicates*, on page 91. We give up the benefits of the natural UIAElement traversal. If you use this, you'll have to pepper your code with manual delays and you won't receive specific UIAElementNil objects as sentinels to help you understand why a query failed.

---

2.   https://github.com/jaykz52/mechanic/

Still, it's a good tool to try out and it comes with some nice utility methods. The concepts behind jQuery revolutionized JavaScript web development, and this library brings similar concepts to UI Automation.

Building Projects with xctool

Although this doesn't relate to UI Automation directly, the xctool command-line utility by the Facebook development team can help simplify the massive output dump from the xcodebuild command that we saw in Section 10.1, *Practicing with the Raw Commands*, on page 165.[3] It's a drop-in replacement for xcodebuild and it generates output like this:

```
$ xctool.sh build -project NearbyMe.xcodeproj -scheme NearbyMeUITests

=== BUILD ===

  xcodebuild build build
    NearbyMe / NearbyMe (Debug)
      ~ Check dependencies (295 ms)
      ...
      ~ Generate NearbyMe.app.dSYM (54 ms)
      ~ CodeSign NearbyMe.app (203 ms)

** BUILD SUCCEEDED ** (1226 ms)
```

You can use a configuration file in the project directory to define default parameters, and it even helps you run your unit tests. This tool is hard to beat and is worth the effort to set up in your tool chain.

Command-Line Power with Bwoken

Bwoken, by the team at Bendyworks, aims to be a one-stop shop for running your UI Automation tests from the command line.[4] Place your test files in specific directories, and Bwoken builds your app and runs against the appropriate device family. You can point it at libraries like Tuneup JS and it will automatically pull them down and set them up. If you're a fan of Coffee-Script, then you'll be happy to know that it will automatically convert test files written in CoffeeScript to JavaScript for you on the fly, too.

To top it all off, it will consume and reformat the UI Automation output to help you figure out what it's doing (see the following figure).

---

3. https://github.com/facebook/xctool
4. http://bendyworks.github.com/bwoken/

```
iphone   favorites.js
Start:   Favoriting a repository
Debug:   tap tableViews["Repositories"].cells["CITravis by Travis-ci"]
Debug:   tap navigationBar.rightButton
Debug:   tap actionSheet.elements["Add"]
Debug:   tap navigationBar.leftButton
Debug:   tap navigationBar.elements["Favorites"]
Debug:   navigationBar.elements["Favorites"].scrollToVisible
Debug:   tap navigationBar.elements["All"]
Pass:    Favoriting a repository
```

Figure 66—Readable output of Bwoken

The trade-off is that it officially supports a more recent version of Ruby than the one that comes with OS X. If you're a maven at Homebrew and you were thinking of writing your own test-runner for UI Automation scripts with a convention-over-configuration style, definitely give this a look.[5]

cisimple

Last, but certainly not least, cisimple is a cloud service that offers continuous integration for your project by executing your UI Automation tests.[6,7] Set it up to listen to your project repository, and it will pull down, build, and run all your tests after each commit. You'll be notified if anything breaks, and you can even download a video recording of the session as the UI Automation scripts run.

As its name implies, it is simple to set up for your projects. Additionally, the team is committed to working and playing smart within Apple's rules for both independent and enterprise developers. Give this a look.

These tools can help you take your UI Automation workflow to the next level, but UI Automation isn't the only game in town. Now let's look at some other tools that can help in the bug hunt.

11.2 Testing outside the Box

As a part of Apple's SDK, UI Automation brings unique advantages. There is nothing extra to install to get it to work, and we can leverage the close tie to

---

5. https://github.com/mxcl/homebrew
6. https://www.cisimple.com
7. http://www.martinfowler.com/articles/continuousIntegration.html

Instruments, as we saw in Chapter 7, *Automating Performance Tests*, on page 101. But that doesn't mean it's always the best tool for the job.

There are two key reasons you might want to consider the resources discussed here: you or your team are already familiar with languages and protocols used to test on other platforms, or you have additional needs that the sandboxed UI Automation instrument cannot meet.

Writing Tests in Ruby and Cucumber with Frank

Developed as an internal project at ThoughtWorks and now publicly maintained by Pete Hodgson, Frank is one of my favorite UI Automation alternatives for full-stack integration testing.[8] It uses Ruby at its core and comes with Cucumber, the popular natural-language layer.[9]

Frank works by injecting a special web server as a static library into your app at link time. This "frankified" build of your app exposes its UI through that web server. If you connect to it with a web browser, you'll see the Symbiote tool that lets you explore the current state of the UI to help you create selector queries that locate elements on the screen. Once you have tests written with Frank, you can use the cloud-based testing service Calabash as a plug-in to run them, just like you can run UI Automation tests with cisimple.[10]

Once the app is "frankified" and you start writing test steps in Ruby, you can string those test steps together using the natural-language syntax of Cucumber, like so:

```
Feature: Result not found
Scenario: Try to find coffee
  Given I launch the app
  When I tap on the search term "coffee"
  Then I see an alert with title "Not found"
```

Expressing the intent of your tests in Cucumber is worth an entire book of its own. When used properly, the natural-language script helps communicate with nontechnical stakeholders in a project. It's a skill that requires explicit effort to keep these scripts fresh and written in the language of the problem domain that everyone agrees on. Read *The Cucumber Book: Behaviour-Driven Development for Testers and Developers [WH11]* for more information.

The catch is that you must be comfortable installing RubyGems on the machine that will run the tests. Some enterprise environments may balk at

---

8. http://testingwithfrank.com
9. http://cukes.info
10. http://calaba.sh

this. Also, note that, because of the injected web server, your "frankified" app is not the same bundle you release to users. In my experience this isn't a problem, but as we discussed in Section 8.4, *Hiding Test-Setup Code from Release*, on page 139, you must pay attention to the differences between your test and release environments. If you have a very complex Xcode workspace setup, you'll need to make sure you stay out of the way of the web server that gets injected into your app.

Functional Testing in Objective-C with KIF

KIF, which stands for "Keep It Functional," was created by Square and lets you write your automation tests in straight Objective-C.[11] It's a novel approach that reduces the number of layers and services needed to test your application.

Here's an example scenario:

```
@implementation KIFTestScenario (EXAdditions)

+ (id)scenarioToLogIn;
{
    KIFTestScenario *scenario = [KIFTestScenario
            scenarioWithDescription:@"Test that a user can successfully log in."];
    [scenario addStep:[KIFTestStep stepToReset]];
    [scenario addStepsFromArray:[KIFTestStep stepsToGoToLoginPage]];
    [scenario addStep:[KIFTestStep stepToEnterText:@"user@example.com"
                    intoViewWithAccessibilityLabel:@"Login User Name"]];
    [scenario addStep:[KIFTestStep stepToEnterText:@"thisismypassword"
                    intoViewWithAccessibilityLabel:@"Login Password"]];
    [scenario addStep:[KIFTestStep stepToTapViewWithAccessibilityLabel:@"Log In"]];

    // Verify that the login succeeded
    [scenario addStep:[KIFTestStep
                    stepToWaitForTappableViewWithAccessibilityLabel:@"Welcome"]];

    return scenario;
}

@end
```

If you don't mind the verbosity of Objective-C, you'll enjoy the fact that your tests run right inside your application process so you can do more complex application manipulation on the fly. You also get compile-time checking of your test code for free!

---

11. https://github.com/square/KIF

Speaking the WebDriver Protocol with Appium

In the web-development world, WebDriver is a very common protocol for developers and QA teams to script interactions with web applications. Appium brings that to iOS by wrapping the low-level UI Automation private framework with a WebDriver layer.[12] That means your team can reuse the knowledge and workflow of tools like Selenium, or even write a custom language-adapter layer that speaks the WebDriver protocol.

Appium is built on top of the Sauce Labs integration-testing service in the cloud. You can have that service watch your project and automatically run your tests—like cisimple but without using UI Automation. There are always risks when adding layers of complexity, but if your team has a lot of experience with the WebDriver protocol, then this is worth a look.

Distributed Automation Recording with Test Studio

Telerik's Test Studio takes a radically different approach.[13] Rather than depend on developers or QA professionals to write test scripts, Test Studio lets anyone record and play back test activities. The recordings can be sent back and attached to bug reports or collected to run at a later time.

Like Frank, it works by injecting a static library into the app. But it also uses a companion native application that communicates with your app through URL protocols. Say you have a beta tester who has Test Studio installed on a device. When that beta tester receives an ad hoc build of your app, he can trigger the recording through the Test Studio app and even manage the resulting script before sending it back to you.

The ability to distribute the responsibility for creating tests is quite unique, and the tool does much more, like capturing crash reports and other user feedback. The disadvantage is that the capture/playback paradigm can yield brittle tests. The tool tries to address this by helping you extract common steps, but I wouldn't use this as my sole source of automation tests. I recommend crafting a reliable and well-factored suite of test scripts by hand as a first line of defense. A tool like Test Studio could be an excellent complement to those scripts.

Regardless of what third-party tools you use, much of what we've walked through still applies: resetting application state, controlling external dependencies, and organizing your tests to minimize brittleness. Whatever tools

---

12. http://appium.io
13. http://www.telerik.com/automated-testing-tools/ios-testing

you choose, this is your opportunity to put the machine to work finding bugs to help you build reliable applications for your users.

But Wait—There's More!

Congratulations. You've made it to the end of this book, but your journey is just beginning. Testing iOS applications is not easy. Every app brings its own challenges, whether you are integrating with complicated external services or you have radically different layouts between device types. I hope the experiences in these chapters help you break down the problems into solvable pieces. Use these skills to hunt bugs and raise your confidence that you've wired everything up correctly.

Thank you for reading. I am honored to be a part of your testing journey. Go and make applications that solve tough problems—and write tests so the machine helps you solve yours.

Bibliography

[AD12]   Chris Adamson and Bill Dudney. *iOS SDK Development*. The Pragmatic Bookshelf, Raleigh, NC and Dallas, TX, 2012.

[Dal11]   Mark Dalrymple. *Advanced Mac OS X Programming: The Big Nerd Ranch Guide*. Big Nerd Ranch Guides, Atlanta, GA, 2011.

[Kle12]   Ben Klemens. *21st Century C*. O'Reilly & Associates, Inc., Sebastopol, CA, 2012.

[Lee12]   Graham Lee. *Test-Driven iOS Development*. Addison-Wesley, Reading, MA, 2012.

[Sog09]   Sal Soghoian. *Apple Training Series: AppleScript 1-2-3*. Peachpit Press, Berkeley, CA, 2009.

[Ste12]   Daniel H. Steinberg. *Test Driving iOS Development With Kiwi*. Dim Sum Thinking, http://dimsumthinking.com/, 2012.

[WD11]   Paul Warren and Matt Drance. *iOS Recipes: Tips and Tricks for Awesome iPhone and iPad Apps*. The Pragmatic Bookshelf, Raleigh, NC and Dallas, TX, 2011.

[WH11]   Matt Wynne and Aslak Hellesøy. *The Cucumber Book: Behaviour-Driven Development for Testers and Developers*. The Pragmatic Bookshelf, Raleigh, NC and Dallas, TX, 2011.

[Zar12]   Marcus S. Zarra. *Core Data: Data Storage and Management for iOS, OS X, and iCloud*. The Pragmatic Bookshelf, Raleigh, NC and Dallas, TX, Second, 2012.

Index

Learn iOS and Mac OS X

Get a solid grounding on development for iOS, or discover the the coolest, most helpful tricks and tips in Mac OS X.

iOS SDK Development

Since the iPhone's launch in 2008, the iOS platform has added two new device families, thousands of new APIs, new tools and programming practices, and hundreds of thousands of new apps. Yours can be one of them. This book guides you through the state of the art of iOS development, including the radically overhauled Xcode 4 toolchain, the iOS 6 SDK, and the new iPhone 5. You'll accelerate your development with new tools like Storyboards, practice on new APIs like the Twitter framework, and learn the latest features of the Objective-C programming language.

Chris Adamson and Bill Dudney
(296 pages) ISBN: 9781934356944. $35
http://pragprog.com/book/adios

Mac Kung Fu (2nd edition)

Squeeze every drop of juice from OS X with over 400 quick and easy tips, tricks, hints and hacks in *Mac Kung Fu: Second Edition*. Exploit secret settings and hidden apps, push built-in tools to the limit, radically personalize your Mac experience, and make "it just works" even better. In addition to core OS X technologies, this significantly revised and expanded update to the best-selling first edition dissects new OS X Mountain Lion tools such as iCloud, Notifications, Reminders, and Calendar.

See *The Unofficial Apple Weblog* review here

Keir Thomas
(424 pages) ISBN: 9781937785079. $39
http://pragprog.com/book/ktmack2

More for iOS

Get up to speed with the latest version of Core Data and more.

Core Data (2nd edition)

Core Data is Apple's recommended way to persist data: it's easy to use, built-in, and integrated with iCloud. It's intricate, powerful, and necessary—and this book is your guide to harnessing its power.

Learn fundamental Core Data principles such as thread and memory management, discover how to use Core Data in your iPhone, iPad, and OS X projects by using NSPredicate to filter data, and see how to add iCloud to your applications.

Marcus S. Zarra
(256 pages) ISBN: 9781937785086. $33
http://pragprog.com/book/mzcd2

iOS Recipes

Take your iPhone and iPad apps to the next level. You've seen cool features and tricks in other apps, but haven't had the time to really look into how they're done. We've got the answers for you. This book walks you through clean, reusable solutions to a wide variety of problems and patterns common to iOS development with Cocoa Touch and Objective-C. With these recipes in your arsenal, your next apps will be more polished and more maintainable than ever.

Written for and tested on iOS 4 and Xcode 4.

Paul Warren and Matt Drance
(224 pages) ISBN: 9781934356746. $33
http://pragprog.com/book/cdirec

The Joy of Math and Programming

Rediscover the joy and fascinating weirdness of pure mathematics, or get your kids started programming in JavaScript.

Good Math

Mathematics is beautiful—and it can be fun and exciting as well as practical. *Good Math* is your guide to some of the most intriguing topics from two thousand years of mathematics: from Egyptian fractions to Turing machines; from the real meaning of numbers to proof trees, group symmetry, and mechanical computation. If you've ever wondered what lay beyond the proofs you struggled to complete in high school geometry, or what limits the capabilities of the computer on your desk, this is the book for you.

Mark C. Chu-Carroll
(282 pages) ISBN: 9781937785338. $34
http://pragprog.com/book/mcmath

3D Game Programming for Kids

You know what's even better than playing games? Creating your own. Even if you're an absolute beginner, this book will teach you how to make your own online games with interactive examples. You'll learn programming using nothing more than a browser, and see cool, 3D results as you type. You'll learn real-world programming skills in a real programming language: JavaScript, the language of the web. You'll be amazed at what you can do as you build interactive worlds and fun games.

Chris Strom
(250 pages) ISBN: 9781937785444. $36
http://pragprog.com/book/csjava

Seven Databases, Seven Languages

There's so much new to learn with the latest crop of NoSQL databases. And instead of learning a language a year, how about seven?

Seven Databases in Seven Weeks

Data is getting bigger and more complex by the day, and so are your choices in handling it. From traditional RDBMS to newer NoSQL approaches, *Seven Databases in Seven Weeks* takes you on a tour of some of the hottest open source databases today. In the tradition of Bruce A. Tate's *Seven Languages in Seven Weeks*, this book goes beyond your basic tutorial to explore the essential concepts at the core of each technology.

Eric Redmond and Jim R. Wilson
(354 pages) ISBN: 9781934356920. $35
http://pragprog.com/book/rwdata

Seven Languages in Seven Weeks

You should learn a programming language every year, as recommended by *The Pragmatic Programmer*. But if one per year is good, how about *Seven Languages in Seven Weeks*? In this book you'll get a hands-on tour of Clojure, Haskell, Io, Prolog, Scala, Erlang, and Ruby. Whether or not your favorite language is on that list, you'll broaden your perspective of programming by examining these languages side-by-side. You'll learn something new from each, and best of all, you'll learn how to learn a language quickly.

Bruce A. Tate
(330 pages) ISBN: 9781934356593. $34.95
http://pragprog.com/book/btlang

Be Agile

Don't just "do" agile; you want to *be* agile. We'll show you how.

Agile in a Flash

The best agile book isn't a book: *Agile in a Flash* is a unique deck of index cards that fit neatly in your pocket. You can tape them to the wall. Spread them out on your project table. Get stains on them over lunch. These cards are meant to be used, not just read.

Jeff Langr and Tim Ottinger
(110 pages) ISBN: 9781934356715. $15
http://pragprog.com/book/olag

The Agile Samurai

Here are three simple truths about software development:

1. You can't gather all the requirements up front. 2. The requirements you do gather will change. 3. There is always more to do than time and money will allow.

Those are the facts of life. But you can deal with those facts (and more) by becoming a fierce software-delivery professional, capable of dispatching the most dire of software projects and the toughest delivery schedules with ease and grace.

Jonathan Rasmusson
(280 pages) ISBN: 9781934356586. $34.95
http://pragprog.com/book/jtrap

Tinker, Tailor, Solder, and DIY!

Get into the DIY spirit with Raspberry Pi or Arduino. Who knows what you'll build next...

Raspberry Pi

The Raspberry Pi is a $35, full-blown micro computer that runs Linux. Use its video, audio, network, and digital I/O to create media centers, web servers, interfaces to external hardware—you name it. And this book gives you everything you need to get started.

Maik Schmidt
(149 pages) ISBN: 9781937785048. $17
http://pragprog.com/book/msraspi

Arduino

Arduino is an open-source platform that makes DIY electronics projects easier than ever. Even if you have no electronics experience, you'll be creating your first gadgets within a few minutes. Step-by-step instructions show you how to build a universal remote, a motion-sensing game controller, and many other fun, useful projects. This book has now been updated for Arduino 1.0, with revised code, examples, and screenshots throughout. We've changed all the book's examples and added new examples showing how to use the Arduino IDE's new features.

Maik Schmidt
(272 pages) ISBN: 9781934356661. $35
http://pragprog.com/book/msard

Kick Your Career up a Notch

Ready to blog or promote yourself for real? Time to refocus your personal priorities? We've got you covered.

Technical Blogging

Technical Blogging is the first book to specifically teach programmers, technical people, and technically-oriented entrepreneurs how to become successful bloggers. There is no magic to successful blogging; with this book you'll learn the techniques to attract and keep a large audience of loyal, regular readers and leverage this popularity to achieve your goals.

Antonio Cangiano
(288 pages) ISBN: 9781934356883. $33
http://pragprog.com/book/actb

The Developer's Code

You're already a great coder, but awesome coding chops aren't always enough to get you through your toughest projects. You need these 50+ nuggets of wisdom. Veteran programmers: reinvigorate your passion for developing web applications. New programmers: here's the guidance you need to get started. With this book, you'll think about your job in new and enlightened ways.

This title is also available as an audio book.

Ka Wai Cheung
(160 pages) ISBN: 9781934356791. $29
http://pragprog.com/book/kcdc

The Pragmatic Bookshelf

The Pragmatic Bookshelf features books written by developers for developers. The titles continue the well-known Pragmatic Programmer style and continue to garner awards and rave reviews. As development gets more and more difficult, the Pragmatic Programmers will be there with more titles and products to help you stay on top of your game.

Visit Us Online

This Book's Home Page
http://pragprog.com/book/jptios
Source code from this book, errata, and other resources. Come give us feedback, too!

Register for Updates
http://pragprog.com/updates
Be notified when updates and new books become available.

Join the Community
http://pragprog.com/community
Read our weblogs, join our online discussions, participate in our mailing list, interact with our wiki, and benefit from the experience of other Pragmatic Programmers.

New and Noteworthy
http://pragprog.com/news
Check out the latest pragmatic developments, new titles and other offerings.

Save on the eBook

Save on the eBook versions of this title. Owning the paper version of this book entitles you to purchase the electronic versions at a terrific discount.

PDFs are great for carrying around on your laptop—they are hyperlinked, have color, and are fully searchable. Most titles are also available for the iPhone and iPod touch, Amazon Kindle, and other popular e-book readers.

Buy now at *http://pragprog.com/coupon*

Contact Us

Online Orders:	*http://pragprog.com/catalog*
Customer Service:	*support@pragprog.com*
International Rights:	*translations@pragprog.com*
Academic Use:	*academic@pragprog.com*
Write for Us:	*http://pragprog.com/write-for-us*
Or Call:	+1 800-699-7764

CPSIA information can be obtained at www.ICGtesting.com
Printed in the USA
LVOW02s1948270913

354472LV00040B/244/P

9 781937 785529